Retirement Reimagined: Empowering Strategies for Financial Freedom After 60

Author: Cathleen L. Fedele

© Copyright 2025 Cathleen L. Fedele

All rights reserved. No part of this guide may be reproduced, transmitted, or distributed in any form or by any means without permission in writing from the publisher except in the case of brief quotations embodied in critical articles or reviews.

Table of Contents

Contents

Introduction: Embracing Your Second Act 12

Chapter 1: The New Reality of Retirement 18

Chapter 2: Facing Financial Facts Without Fear 27

    Assessing the Average Savings of Those Over 60 27

        A Stark Reality Check 27

        The Growing Longevity Gap 28

        Economic Fluctuations and Market Volatility 28

        The Shift from Defined Benefit to Defined Contribution Plans 29

    Encouraging an Honest Look at Personal Finances Without Intimidation 29

        The Power of Transparency 29

        Overcoming Emotional Barriers 31

        Building Financial Literacy 31

    Introducing the Importance of Proactive Financial Planning 32

        Taking Charge of Your Financial Future 32

        The Role of Diversification in Investment 34

        Maximizing Social Security and Pension Benefits 35

        Planning for Unexpected Expenses 35

        Leveraging Technology for Financial Management ... 36

        The Psychological Benefits of Financial Planning 37

    Practical Steps to Begin Your Financial Assessment 38

        Step 1: Gather Your Financial Information 38

        Step 2: Create a Net Worth Statement 38

Step 3: Analyze Your Income and Expenses 39

Step 4: Identify Financial Goals 39

Step 5: Develop an Action Plan 40

Step 6: Monitor and Adjust 40

Embracing Proactive Financial Planning 40

The Benefits of Early and Continuous Planning 40

Building a Support System 41

Emphasizing Continuous Education 42

Real-Life Success Stories: Overcoming Financial Challenges 42

Maria's Journey to Financial Stability 42

Tom's Path to Debt-Free Retirement 43

Linda's Strategic Investment Approach 44

Embracing the Journey Ahead 44

Taking the First Step 45

Building Momentum 45

The Path Forward 46

Final Thoughts 46

Reflective Questions 47

Chapter 3: Triumphs After 60: Stories of Success 49

Maria's Path to Financial Independence 49

Starting Fresh with Financial Literacy 49

Tom's Entrepreneurial Leap 50

From Engineer to Successful Business Owner 50

Linda's Strategic Investment Approach 51

Maximizing Retirement Funds Through Smart Investments 51

George's Debt-Free Retirement 52
   Eliminating Debt to Enhance Financial Well-Being 52
Emma's Journey to Financial Resilience 53
   Leveraging Community Resources and Support 53
Lessons from These Triumphs 54
It's Never Too Late to Make a Positive Change 55
Chapter 4: Supercharging Your Savings: Proven Techniques 57
   1. Smart Investments: Making Your Money Work for You 57
     a. Diversify Your Portfolio 57
     b. Focus on Dividend-Paying Stocks 58
     c. Utilize Low-Cost Index Funds and ETFs 58
     d. Consider Annuities for Guaranteed Income 59
   2. Effective Budgeting: Maximizing Every Dollar 59
     a. Track Your Spending 60
     b. Create a Realistic Budget 60
     c. Reduce Unnecessary Expenses 60
     d. Plan for Major Expenses 61
   3. Debt Management: Eliminating Financial Burdens 61
     a. Assess Your Debt Situation 61
     b. Develop a Debt Repayment Plan 62
     c. Consolidate and Refinance 62
     d. Avoid Accumulating New Debt 63
   4. Step-by-Step Guidance for Boosting Your Savings 63
     Step 1: Conduct a Financial Assessment 63
     Step 2: Set Clear Financial Goals 64
     Step 3: Create and Implement a Budget 64

Step 4: Optimize Your Investments 65

Step 5: Manage and Eliminate Debt 65

Step 6: Increase Income Streams 65

Step 7: Leverage Technology and Resources 66

5. Tailoring Strategies for Those Over 60 66

a. Prioritize Stability and Security 66

b. Maximize Social Security Benefits 67

c. Plan for Healthcare Expenses 67

d. Consider Downsizing 68

e. Stay Engaged and Informed 68

Empowering Your Financial Future 69

Chapter 5: Unlocking the Full Potential of Social Security and Medicare 71

1. Maximizing Social Security Benefits 71

a. Understanding Your Social Security Benefits 71

b. Strategies to Maximize Benefits 72

c. Work Longer if Possible 73

2. Navigating the Complexities of Medicare 74

a. Understanding Medicare Parts 74

b. Enrolling in Medicare 75

c. Choosing the Right Medicare Plan 75

d. Understanding Medicare Costs 77

3. Timing and Coordination for Optimal Results 77

a. Coordinating Social Security and Medicare Enrollment 77

b. Strategic Claiming of Social Security Benefits 78

c. Maximizing Lifetime Benefits 78

d. Leveraging Professional Advice 79

4. Practical Steps to Unlock the Full Potential 79
  Step 1: Assess Your Current Situation 80
  Step 2: Develop a Comprehensive Plan 80
  Step 3: Enroll in Medicare on Time 80
  Step 4: Optimize Social Security Claiming Strategy 80
  Step 5: Integrate Social Security and Medicare into Your Financial Plan 81
  Step 6: Regularly Review and Adjust Your Strategy 81
5. Overcoming Common Challenges 82
  a. Navigating Complex Regulations 82
  b. Managing Health-Related Issues 82
  c. Avoiding Common Pitfalls 83
6. Case Studies: Real-Life Examples 83
  Case Study 1: Sarah's Strategic Delaying of Benefits 83
  Case Study 2: John's Comprehensive Medicare Plan 84
  Case Study 3: Emily and Michael's Spousal Coordination . 84
7. Additional Tips for Optimal Results 85
  a. Utilize Online Tools and Resources 85
  b. Stay Proactive with Communication 85
  c. Consider Professional Advocacy 86
  d. Plan for the Unexpected 86
8. Empowering Your Retirement with Knowledge and Strategy 86

Chapter 6: New Ventures: Earning Income on Your Terms 89
  1. Exploring Part-Time Work and Entrepreneurial Opportunities 89
    a. The Appeal of Part-Time Work 89

b. Entrepreneurial Opportunities 90

2. Turning Hobbies and Passions into Profitable
Endeavors... 91

    a. Monetizing Your Passions 91

    b. Leveraging Technology 92

3. Balancing Work with Leisure in the Golden Years 93

    a. Prioritizing Work-Life Balance 93

    b. Integrating Work with Personal Interests 94

    c. Embracing Flexibility 94

4. Success Stories: Real-Life Examples 95

    a. Grace's Handmade Jewelry Business 95

    b. Robert's Consulting Firm 95

5. Tips for Success in New Ventures 96

    a. Start Small and Scale Gradually 96

    b. Network and Connect 96

    c. Stay Organized and Manage Time Effectively 96

    d. Seek Continuous Learning 96

Crafting a Fulfilling Retirement 97

Chapter 7: Living Well for Less 99

1. Strategies for Reducing Expenses Without Sacrificing
Quality of Life 99

    a. Create a Realistic Budget 99

    b. Prioritize Needs Over Wants 100

2. Tips on Downsizing, Smart Shopping, and Cost-Effective
Living 100

    a. Downsizing Your Living Space 100

    b. Smart Shopping Practices 101

    c. Embracing Cost-Effective Living 101

  3. Embracing a Lifestyle That Prioritizes Fulfillment Over Materialism 102

    a. Focus on Experiences 102

    b. Cultivate Relationships 103

    c. Practice Minimalism 103

  4. Real-Life Examples: Living Well for Less 104

    a. Betty's Smart Budgeting 104

    b. George's Downsizing Journey 104

    c. Linda's Minimalist Lifestyle 104

  5. Tips for Sustaining Cost-Effective Living 105

    a. Regular Financial Check-Ups 105

    b. Stay Informed and Educated 105

    c. Embrace Creativity and Innovation 106

  Living a Fulfilling and Cost-Effective Retirement 106

Chapter 8: Your Support Network: Resources to Help You Thrive 109

  1. Organizations and Programs Offering Assistance to Seniors 109

    a. Government Programs 110

    b. Non-Profit Organizations 111

    c. Community-Based Organizations 112

    d. Healthcare Organizations 113

  2. Accessing Community Resources and Support Groups ... 113

    a. How to Find and Access Resources 113

    b. Joining Support Groups 114

    c. Leveraging Technology for Connection 115

3. The Importance of Building a Network for Financial and Emotional Support 116

    a. Financial Support...116

    b. Emotional Support 117

4. Practical Tips for Building and Maintaining Your Support Network 118

    a. Get Involved in Community Activities............................118

    b. Pursue Lifelong Learning..118

    c. Stay Connected with Family and Friends 119

    d. Utilize Technology to Enhance Connections.................119

    e. Seek Professional Networking Opportunities 120

5. Leveraging Available Resources to Enhance Your Network 120

    a. Financial Assistance Programs 120

    b. Health and Wellness Programs.......................................121

    c. Educational and Skill Development Resources 121

6. The Role of Emotional Support in Financial Well-Being... 122

    a. Reducing Financial Stress...123

    b. Enhancing Overall Well-Being...123

    c. Building Resilience Through Support 124

7. Maintaining and Strengthening Your Support Network..124

    a. Regular Communication...124

    b. Expanding Your Network 125

    c. Leveraging Technology...125

    d. Investing Time and Effort...126

8. Real-Life Examples: Thriving with a Support Network......126

    a. Susan's Engagement with Local Organizations 126

    b. David's Use of Online Communities 127

    c. Linda's Volunteer Work 127

  9. Final Thoughts: Empowering Yourself Through a Strong Support Network 127

Conclusion: Stepping Confidently into the Future 130

  Key Takeaways 130

    1. Understanding the New Reality of Retirement 130

    2. Facing Financial Facts Without Fear 130

    3. Triumphs After 60: Stories of Success 131

    4. Supercharging Your Savings: Proven Techniques 131

    5. Unlocking the Full Potential of Social Security and Medicare 131

    6. New Ventures: Earning Income on Your Terms 131

    7. Living Well for Less 132

    8. Your Support Network: Resources to Help You Thrive 132

  Encouraging Ongoing Action 132

  Reinforcing Empowerment and Self-Sufficiency 133

  Embracing Future Opportunities 133

    Take the Leap 133

    Final Inspiration 134

Introduction: Embracing Your Second Act

A New Chapter Begins

Welcome to *Retirement Reimagined: Empowering Strategies for Financial Freedom After 60*. If you're reading this, chances are you're standing at the threshold of a significant life transition. Whether you're approaching retirement, already retired, or simply contemplating the future, this book is designed with you in mind.

Retirement is often portrayed as a time of leisure—a well-deserved reward after decades of hard work. While rest and relaxation are undoubtedly important, today's retirees are finding that this phase of life can offer so much more. It's a time to rediscover passions, embark on new adventures, and, crucially, take control of your financial destiny.

The Changing Landscape of Retirement

The concept of retirement has evolved dramatically over the past few decades. No longer is it a uniform experience defined by a gold watch and a pension. Today's retirees are more active and engaged, and, in many cases, continue to contribute to the workforce in meaningful ways. However, with these changes come new challenges.

Consider these facts:

- **An Aging Nation**: The proportion of the U.S. population aged 60 and over is growing rapidly. This demographic shift has profound implications for social services, healthcare, and the economy.

- **Financial Uncertainty**: Many individuals over 60 find themselves with less savings than anticipated. Economic fluctuations, changing employment landscapes, and longer life expectancies mean that traditional retirement planning may no longer suffice.
- **Extended Careers**: More people are choosing or needing to work beyond the traditional retirement age. Whether driven by financial necessity or the desire to stay active, the lines between working years and retirement are increasingly blurred.

Why This Book Matters

Amidst this backdrop, it's clear that navigating retirement today requires a fresh perspective and a proactive approach. That's where this book comes in. Our goal is to equip you with practical strategies, insightful stories, and valuable resources to help you enhance your financial well-being and embrace the opportunities that lie ahead.

Here's what you can expect:

- **Actionable Advice**: We'll delve into proven techniques to boost your retirement funds, manage expenses, and make informed financial decisions tailored to your unique situation.
- **Inspiring Narratives**: Real-life stories of individuals who have successfully transformed their financial outlook after 60 will provide both inspiration and practical lessons.
- **Resource Guide**: Information on organizations, programs, and tools available to support seniors in achieving financial security and overall well-being.

A Conversation, Not a Lecture

This book is intended to be a conversation—a dialogue between friends sharing experiences and knowledge. We aim to present information in a respectful, straightforward manner without overwhelming jargon or condescension. Financial topics can be complex, but they don't have to be intimidating. By breaking down concepts into understandable terms, we hope to empower you to make confident decisions.

Your Journey, Your Choice

It's important to recognize that everyone's journey is unique. There is no one-size-fits-all solution when it comes to retirement planning. Factors such as personal goals, health, family circumstances, and existing financial resources all play a role in shaping your path forward.

Our intention is not to prescribe a specific course of action but to provide a toolkit from which you can draw the strategies that resonate most with you. Whether you're looking to maximize your savings, explore new income streams, or adjust your lifestyle to align with your resources, this book offers guidance to help you make informed choices.

Overcoming Obstacles Together

We also acknowledge the emotional and psychological aspects of financial planning. Concerns about money can evoke feelings of anxiety, uncertainty, and even shame. It's crucial to approach these topics with compassion and understanding.

Remember, you are not alone. Many face similar challenges, and there is strength in community and shared experiences. Throughout this book, we'll address common obstacles and offer encouragement to help you overcome them.

The Power of Taking Action

Knowledge is empowering, but action is transformative. As you read through the chapters, we encourage you to actively engage with the material:

- **Reflect**: Consider how the information applies to your personal circumstances.
- **Plan**: Identify specific steps you can take to improve your financial situation.
- **Act**: Implement strategies incrementally, celebrating small victories along the way.

Change doesn't happen overnight, but consistent effort can lead to significant progress. Even modest adjustments can have a meaningful impact on your financial health and overall quality of life.

Looking Ahead with Optimism

While it's essential to acknowledge the challenges that come with aging and retirement, it's equally important to focus on the opportunities. This stage of life can be incredibly fulfilling—a time to pursue passions, deepen relationships, and contribute to your community in new ways.

Financial security plays a key role in enabling these experiences. By taking proactive steps now, you can create a solid foundation that supports not just your needs but also your dreams and aspirations.

Join the Journey

Thank you for choosing to spend your time with this book. Your willingness to engage with these topics speaks volumes about your commitment to shaping a positive future for yourself.

As we embark on this journey together, keep an open mind, ask questions, and be gentle with yourself. The road ahead may have its twists and turns, but with the right tools and mindset, you are well-equipped to navigate it successfully.

So, let's turn the page and begin exploring the empowering strategies that await you. Your second act is just beginning, and it's full of potential.

Warm regards,

Cathleen Fedele

A Note on Sources and Accuracy

Throughout this book, we've made every effort to provide accurate, up-to-date information. Statistics and data are drawn from reputable sources available at the time of writing. However, financial landscapes can change rapidly. We encourage you to consult professional advisors and current resources to ensure that you have the most recent information pertinent to your decisions.

How to Use This Book

- **Start Where You Are**: Feel free to read the chapters in order or jump to sections that are most relevant to your immediate concerns.
- **Engage with the Material**: Take notes, highlight passages, and consider discussing insights with friends or family members.
- **Take Action**: Each chapter includes practical steps you can implement. Even small actions can lead to meaningful progress over time.

Chapter 1: The New Reality of Retirement

Embracing a Changing Landscape

Retirement isn't what it used to be. Gone are the days when reaching 65 meant a swift transition into a life of leisure, funded comfortably by a robust pension and substantial savings. Today's retirees are navigating a vastly different terrain—one that is both challenging and rich with opportunities for those willing to adapt and seize the moment.

A Snapshot of Today's Retiree

Let's begin with some eye-opening statistics that paint a picture of the current landscape:

- **An Aging Population**: As of the latest data, approximately 16% of the U.S. population is aged 65 and over—a figure projected to grow significantly in the coming decades. The aging of the Baby Boomer generation is reshaping the demographic makeup of the nation.
- **Extended Work Life**: More than 20% of individuals aged 65 and older are either working or actively looking for work. This is a marked increase from previous generations and reflects a shift in how we perceive aging and employment.
- **Savings Shortfall**: Alarmingly, nearly half of households headed by someone aged 55 and older have no retirement savings at all. For those who do have savings, the median amount is often insufficient to sustain a comfortable retirement over the long term.

Why Are People Working Longer?

Several factors contribute to the trend of extended work lives:

1. **Financial Necessity**: The cost of living continues to rise, and many find that their savings, pensions, and Social Security benefits don't stretch as far as anticipated. Healthcare expenses, in particular, can be a significant burden.
2. **Inadequate Savings**: The shift from employer-funded pensions to employee-funded retirement accounts like 401(k)s has placed more responsibility on individuals to save for their retirement. Unfortunately, not everyone has been able to save enough.
3. **Longevity**: Advances in healthcare mean people are living longer, healthier lives. While this is a positive development, it also means that retirement savings need to last longer, sometimes 20 to 30 years or more.
4. **Desire for Engagement**: Many seniors choose to continue working not out of necessity, but because they enjoy the mental stimulation, social interaction, and sense of purpose that work provides.

Debunking Retirement Myths

It's essential to challenge some common misconceptions about aging and retirement:

- **Myth 1: Retirement Means Complete Withdrawal from Work**

    Retirement doesn't have to be an all-or-nothing proposition. Many find fulfillment in part-time work, consulting, or starting a small business. These avenues not only supplement income but also keep individuals engaged and active.

- **Myth 2: It's Too Late to Improve Financial Health After 60**

    While starting early has its advantages, it's never too late to take steps toward financial improvement. Strategic planning, wise investments, and savvy money management can make a significant difference, even if you start in your 60s.

- **Myth 3: Seniors Aren't Tech-Savvy Enough for Today's Opportunities**

    The digital divide is narrowing. More seniors are embracing technology to manage finances, work remotely, and stay connected. Online platforms offer flexible opportunities that didn't exist for previous generations.

The Evolving Concept of Retirement

Retirement today is less about withdrawing from the workforce and more about transitioning to different kinds of work or lifestyles that align with personal values and passions. This evolution is redefining what it means to be "retired."

- **Encore Careers**: Many are pursuing second careers that are more fulfilling or socially impactful. This shift allows retirees to leverage their experience in new and meaningful ways.
- **Lifelong Learning**: The pursuit of knowledge doesn't stop at a certain age. Educational opportunities—both formal and informal—are more accessible than ever, enabling seniors to acquire

new skills that can lead to new income streams or personal enrichment.

Embracing Opportunities

The challenges faced by today's retirees are undeniable, but so are the opportunities. With the right mindset and strategies, it's possible to navigate this new reality successfully.

- **Financial Literacy**: Understanding personal finance is crucial. Educate yourself about investment options, retirement accounts, and tax implications to make informed decisions.
- **Networking**: Leverage personal and professional networks. Connections can lead to job opportunities, partnerships, or collaborations that enhance both your financial and social well-being.
- **Health and Wellness**: Prioritizing health can reduce medical expenses and improve quality of life. Embracing a healthy lifestyle is an investment in your future self.

A Call to Action

The new reality of retirement calls for proactive engagement. It's about taking control of your financial future, embracing change, and being open to new possibilities. The path may not be the same as it was for previous generations, but it can be just as rewarding—if not more so.

In the chapters that follow, we'll delve deeper into strategies and stories that illuminate the way forward. You'll discover practical tips to boost your retirement funds, inspiring tales of those who've successfully reinvented their later years, and resources to support you on this journey.

Remember, retirement isn't an end; it's a new beginning. With determination and the right tools, you can create a fulfilling and financially secure future.

Key Takeaways from Chapter 1

- **Retirement Age Is Shifting**: More people are working beyond traditional retirement age due to financial needs, longer life expectancy, and personal fulfillment.
- **Myths Are Meant to Be Broken**: Don't let outdated beliefs limit your potential. It's never too late to improve your financial situation or embark on new ventures.
- **Opportunities Abound**: The modern landscape offers numerous avenues for income, engagement, and growth for those willing to adapt.

A Glimpse into Jane's Journey

To bring these concepts to life, let's look at the story of Jane Thompson, a 62-year-old who found herself at an unexpected crossroads. After dedicating over 35 years to her career as a graphic designer, Jane was laid off due to company downsizing. With limited savings and a modest pension, she faced the daunting prospect of funding her retirement years.

Initially overwhelmed, Jane grappled with anxiety about her financial future. The job market seemed unforgiving, especially for someone her age in a rapidly evolving industry. However, rather than resigning herself to uncertainty, Jane decided to redefine what retirement could mean for her.

Drawing upon her lifelong passion for art and teaching, she began offering art classes in her community. Starting small, she hosted workshops in local community centers and libraries. Her classes focused not just on technique but also on using art as a form of personal expression and stress relief—a concept that resonated deeply with many.

Word of mouth spread quickly. Jane's classes became a staple in the community, attracting not only seniors but adults of all ages seeking a creative outlet. Encouraged by this success, she expanded her offerings by creating online tutorials and webinars. Embracing technology, she set up a simple website and utilized social media to reach a broader audience.

Embracing Technology and New Opportunities

Jane's willingness to learn new skills was instrumental in her success. Despite initial apprehension, she took online courses to familiarize herself with digital tools essential for running an online business. This adaptability not only enhanced her income but also kept her mentally stimulated and engaged with current trends.

Her online classes began attracting international students, opening doors she hadn't imagined possible. The flexibility of an online platform allowed her to work from home, set her own schedule, and connect with a diverse group of people—all while generating a steady income stream.

Impacting Lives Beyond Financial Gains

Beyond the financial benefits, Jane found profound fulfillment in her new venture. She wasn't just teaching art; she was fostering community, inspiring others to explore their creativity, and proving that age is no barrier to starting something new. Her story began inspiring others in her network to pursue their passions and consider alternative paths in their own retirement journeys.

Lessons from Jane's Experience

Jane's journey offers valuable insights applicable to many:

1. **Leveraging Existing Skills and Passions**: By combining her expertise in art with a newfound interest in teaching, Jane created a niche that was both personally rewarding and financially viable.
2. **Lifelong Learning**: Embracing new technologies and platforms was crucial. Jane's willingness to learn kept her skills relevant and opened up modern avenues for income.
3. **Community Engagement**: Starting at the local level helped Jane build a supportive network. Community resources can be a powerful springboard for new endeavors.
4. **Resilience and Adaptability**: Jane faced her challenges head-on, adapting to circumstances and finding opportunities within obstacles.

The Broader Implications

Jane's story is not unique. It reflects a growing trend among seniors who are redefining retirement:

- **Entrepreneurship is Ageless**: Seniors are the fastest-growing group of entrepreneurs in the U.S. Experience, networks, and professional skills accumulated over decades can be invaluable assets in starting a business.
- **Contribution to the Economy**: By remaining active in the workforce—whether through traditional employment or entrepreneurial

ventures—seniors contribute significantly to economic growth and innovation.
- **Breaking Stereotypes**: Success stories like Jane's challenge outdated notions about aging, demonstrating that seniors can be tech-savvy, adaptable, and highly productive.

Moving Forward with Confidence

Jane's journey underscores the potential that lies in embracing the new reality of retirement. It's a call to action for others to:

- **Explore Personal Passions**: Retirement can be the perfect time to pursue interests that may have been sidelined during earlier career stages.
- **Seek Out Resources**: Numerous organizations offer support, from small business associations to online learning platforms tailored for seniors.
- **Build a Support Network**: Connecting with like-minded individuals can provide encouragement, ideas, and potential collaborations.

Questions for Reflection

1. **How Do You Envision Your Retirement?**

    Consider what retirement means to you personally. Is it a time for rest, exploration, new challenges, or a combination of these?

2. **What Steps Can You Take Today?**

    Identify immediate actions that can positively impact your financial health and overall well-being.

3. **Who Can Support You on This Journey?**

    Think about friends, family, or professional advisors who can offer guidance and encouragement.

As we continue, keep an open mind and be ready to embrace the possibilities that lie ahead. Your journey is unique, and with the insights and strategies shared in this book, you can navigate the new reality of retirement with confidence and optimism.

Final Thoughts

The landscape of retirement is shifting, and with it comes the opportunity to redefine what these years can look like. Jane's story exemplifies how challenges can be transformed into fulfilling new chapters. By staying open to learning and willing to step outside of comfort zones, it's possible to not only secure financial stability but also achieve personal growth and satisfaction.

As you reflect on your own journey, consider what passions or skills you might cultivate. The path to a rewarding retirement is as unique as each individual, and the possibilities are as vast as your imagination allows.

Chapter 2: Facing Financial Facts Without Fear

Embracing Financial Reality with Confidence

Navigating the financial landscape after 60 can feel like steering a ship through uncharted waters. The statistics may seem daunting, but understanding the numbers and facing them head-on is the first step toward securing a stable and fulfilling retirement. This chapter is dedicated to helping you assess where you stand financially, confront the challenges ahead with clarity, and embrace proactive financial planning with confidence.

Assessing the Average Savings of Those Over 60

A Stark Reality Check

To begin, let's examine the current state of retirement savings among Americans over 60. Recent studies and surveys reveal a mixed picture, highlighting both progress and areas of concern.

- **Median Retirement Savings**: According to a 2023 report by the Federal Reserve, the median retirement savings for households headed by someone aged 60-69 is approximately $120,000. While this may seem substantial, it's important to consider that the average American couple may need between $300,000 to $500,000 to maintain their pre-retirement standard of living.
- **Savings Shortfall**: Nearly 45% of individuals over 60 have less than $100,000 saved for retirement.

This significant portion of the population faces considerable challenges in sustaining their desired lifestyle without additional income streams or financial support.
- **Dependence on Social Security**: For many, Social Security benefits constitute the cornerstone of retirement income. However, these benefits alone are often insufficient to cover all expenses, particularly healthcare costs, housing, and unexpected emergencies.

The Growing Longevity Gap

Advancements in healthcare have extended life expectancy, which is a double-edged sword. On one hand, it's wonderful to enjoy more years of good health and active living. On the other hand, it means that retirement funds must stretch further to cover a longer retirement period.

- **Increased Longevity**: The average life expectancy in the United States has risen to around 81 years. This means that individuals retiring at 65 could potentially spend 20 years or more in retirement, making the sustainability of their savings crucial.
- **Healthcare Costs**: Medical expenses tend to increase with age. The U.S. Department of Health and Human Services estimates that a 65-year-old couple retiring in 2023 may need approximately $300,000 to cover healthcare expenses throughout retirement.

Economic Fluctuations and Market Volatility

The economic environment plays a significant role in retirement planning. Market downturns, inflation, and changes in interest rates can all impact the value of retirement savings.

- **Market Volatility**: Events such as the 2008 financial crisis and the economic impact of the COVID-19 pandemic have underscored the vulnerability of retirement portfolios to sudden market shifts.
- **Inflation Concerns**: Persistent inflation can erode purchasing power, making it essential to invest in assets that can outpace inflation over time.

The Shift from Defined Benefit to Defined Contribution Plans

The transition from traditional pension plans (defined benefit) to 401(k) and other defined contribution plans has placed more responsibility on individuals to manage their retirement savings.

- **Less Employer Support**: With fewer employers offering guaranteed pensions, retirees must rely more heavily on personal savings and investments, increasing the need for financial literacy and planning.
- **Investment Management**: Managing a 401(k) or IRA requires understanding investment options, risk tolerance, and the importance of diversification to protect against market volatility.

Encouraging an Honest Look at Personal Finances Without Intimidation

The Power of Transparency

Facing the reality of your financial situation can be intimidating, but it's a necessary step toward achieving financial security. Embracing transparency with yourself about your finances empowers you to make informed decisions and take control of your future.

1. Conduct a Comprehensive Financial Assessment

Begin by taking stock of your current financial situation. This includes:

- **Assets**: List all your assets, including savings accounts, retirement accounts, real estate, investments, and personal property.
- **Liabilities**: Identify all debts, such as mortgages, car loans, credit card balances, and any other obligations.
- **Income Sources**: Outline all sources of income, including Social Security, pensions, rental income, part-time work, and investment dividends.
- **Expenses**: Track your monthly and annual expenses, distinguishing between essential and discretionary spending.

2. Utilize Financial Tools and Resources

There are numerous tools available to help you assess your financial health without feeling overwhelmed:

- **Budgeting Apps**: Applications like Mint, YNAB (You Need A Budget), and Personal Capital can help you track income and expenses, set budgeting goals, and monitor your financial progress.
- **Retirement Calculators**: Online calculators can estimate how much you need to save for retirement based on your current savings, expected retirement age, and desired lifestyle.
- **Financial Advisors**: Consulting with a certified financial planner can provide personalized insights and strategies tailored to your unique situation.

3. Embrace a Growth Mindset

Approaching your finances with a growth mindset means viewing challenges as opportunities for improvement rather than insurmountable obstacles. This perspective can reduce anxiety and foster a proactive attitude toward financial planning.

Overcoming Emotional Barriers

Financial discussions often come with emotional baggage, such as fear, guilt, or embarrassment. Overcoming these barriers is essential for making sound financial decisions.

1. Acknowledge Your Feelings

It's normal to feel anxious or overwhelmed when confronting financial realities. Acknowledging these emotions can help you address them constructively.

2. Seek Support

Don't hesitate to reach out to trusted friends, family members, or support groups. Sharing your concerns can provide emotional relief and practical advice.

3. Focus on Solutions

Shift your focus from the problems to potential solutions. Identifying actionable steps can transform feelings of helplessness into a sense of agency and control.

Building Financial Literacy

Understanding financial concepts is key to managing your retirement effectively. Investing time in building your financial literacy can demystify complex topics and empower you to make informed choices.

1. Educational Resources

Leverage books, online courses, webinars, and workshops focused on retirement planning, investment strategies, and personal finance management.

2. Stay Informed

Keep abreast of financial news and trends that may impact your retirement. Subscribing to reputable financial publications or following financial experts can provide valuable insights.

3. Ask Questions

Don't hesitate to ask questions, whether it's to a financial advisor, a knowledgeable friend, or through online forums. Clarifying doubts can enhance your understanding and confidence.

Introducing the Importance of Proactive Financial Planning

Taking Charge of Your Financial Future

Proactive financial planning is about anticipating future needs and taking steps today to ensure a secure and comfortable retirement. It's a dynamic process that adapts to changes in your life circumstances, economic conditions, and personal goals.

1. Setting Clear Financial Goals

Define what you want to achieve in retirement. Goals can range from maintaining a certain standard of living, traveling, supporting family members, or leaving a legacy. Clear goals provide direction and motivation for your financial planning efforts.

2. Creating a Detailed Plan

A comprehensive financial plan outlines the steps necessary to achieve your retirement goals. This includes:

- **Saving and Investment Strategies**: Determine how much you need to save, where to invest your funds, and how to diversify your portfolio to balance growth and risk.
- **Budgeting for Retirement**: Develop a realistic budget that accounts for expected income and expenses. This helps ensure that your spending aligns with your savings and income sources.
- **Debt Management**: Formulate a strategy to reduce or eliminate debt, which can free up more resources for savings and essential expenses.

3. Risk Management and Insurance

Protecting your assets and income is a critical component of financial planning.

- **Health Insurance**: Ensure you have adequate health coverage to manage medical expenses. Consider options like Medicare supplements or long-term care insurance.
- **Life Insurance**: Evaluate whether life insurance is necessary to support your dependents or cover any outstanding debts.

- **Asset Protection**: Explore ways to safeguard your assets from potential risks, such as market downturns or unexpected expenses.

The Role of Diversification in Investment

Diversification involves spreading your investments across various asset classes to minimize risk. This strategy is particularly important for retirees who may not have the time to recover from significant market losses.

1. Asset Allocation

Allocate your investments among different asset classes, such as stocks, bonds, real estate, and cash equivalents. The right mix depends on your risk tolerance, investment horizon, and financial goals.

2. Rebalancing Your Portfolio

Regularly review and adjust your portfolio to maintain your desired asset allocation. Rebalancing helps ensure that your investments remain aligned with your risk tolerance and financial objectives.

3. Seeking Professional Guidance

Consulting with a financial advisor can provide personalized investment strategies tailored to your unique situation. Advisors can offer insights into market trends, tax-efficient investment options, and strategies to optimize your portfolio.

Maximizing Social Security and Pension Benefits

Understanding how to optimize Social Security and pension benefits is crucial for maximizing your retirement income.

1. Timing Your Benefits

Deciding when to start taking Social Security benefits can significantly impact your lifetime income. Delaying benefits beyond your full retirement age can result in higher monthly payments.

2. Coordinating with Spousal Benefits

If you're married, coordinating Social Security benefits with your spouse can enhance your overall income. Strategies such as spousal benefits, survivor benefits, and claiming at different times can optimize your household's financial situation.

3. Understanding Pension Options

If you have a pension, it's important to understand the payout options available, such as lump-sum distributions or annuity payments. Evaluating the pros and cons of each option can help you choose the best path for your financial needs.

Planning for Unexpected Expenses

Unexpected expenses, such as medical emergencies or home repairs, can derail your retirement plans if not properly accounted for.

1. Building an Emergency Fund

Maintain an emergency fund with three to six months' worth of living expenses. This fund acts as a financial cushion, providing peace of mind and stability in case of unforeseen events.

2. Long-Term Care Planning

Consider the potential need for long-term care services, which can be costly. Exploring options like long-term care insurance or setting aside dedicated savings can help mitigate these expenses.

3. Estate Planning

Ensure that your estate is in order by creating a will, establishing trusts, and designating beneficiaries. Proper estate planning can prevent legal complications and ensure that your assets are distributed according to your wishes.

Leveraging Technology for Financial Management

In today's digital age, technology offers numerous tools to streamline financial management and enhance your retirement planning.

1. Online Banking and Budgeting Tools

Utilize online banking platforms and budgeting tools to monitor your finances, track expenses, and manage your investments efficiently.

2. Robo-Advisors

Robo-advisors provide automated, algorithm-driven financial planning services with minimal human intervention. They offer a cost-effective way to manage your investments, especially if you prefer a hands-off approach.

3. Financial Planning Software

Advanced financial planning software can help you model different scenarios, project future income and expenses, and create detailed retirement plans tailored to your goals.

The Psychological Benefits of Financial Planning

Beyond the tangible financial benefits, proactive financial planning offers significant psychological advantages.

1. Reducing Anxiety and Stress

Knowing that you have a plan in place can alleviate worries about the future, allowing you to enjoy your retirement with greater peace of mind.

2. Enhancing Confidence and Control

Taking charge of your financial situation empowers you to make informed decisions, fostering a sense of control and confidence in your ability to manage your retirement effectively.

3. Promoting a Positive Outlook

A well-structured financial plan encourages a positive outlook on retirement, shifting your focus from potential challenges to the opportunities that lie ahead.

Practical Steps to Begin Your Financial Assessment

Step 1: Gather Your Financial Information

Start by collecting all relevant financial documents, including:

- Bank statements
- Retirement account statements (401(k), IRA, etc.)
- Investment portfolios
- Pension statements
- Social Security statements
- Insurance policies
- Mortgage and loan documents
- Monthly bills and receipts

Step 2: Create a Net Worth Statement

Calculate your net worth by subtracting your total liabilities from your total assets. This provides a clear snapshot of your financial standing.

Example:

- **Assets**: $150,000 (savings) + $200,000 (home) + $100,000 (investments) = $450,000
- **Liabilities**: $100,000 (mortgage) + $20,000 (car loan) + $10,000 (credit card debt) = $130,000
- **Net Worth**: $450,000 - $130,000 = $320,000

Step 3: Analyze Your Income and Expenses

List all sources of income and track your monthly and annual expenses. This helps identify areas where you can cut costs or reallocate funds toward savings and investments.

Income Sources:

- Social Security: $2,000/month
- Pension: $1,500/month
- Part-time work: $1,000/month
- Investments: $500/month
- **Total Income**: $5,000/month

Expenses:

- Housing: $1,200/month
- Utilities: $300/month
- Food: $600/month
- Healthcare: $800/month
- Transportation: $400/month
- Entertainment: $200/month
- Miscellaneous: $300/month
- **Total Expenses**: $3,800/month

Surplus: $1,200/month

Step 4: Identify Financial Goals

Define your short-term and long-term financial goals. Examples include:

- **Short-Term Goals**: Paying off high-interest debt, building an emergency fund, and traveling.

- **Long-Term Goals**: Ensuring a comfortable retirement, leaving a legacy, and supporting grandchildren's education.

Step 5: Develop an Action Plan

Create a detailed plan outlining the steps needed to achieve your financial goals. This may involve:

- Increasing savings contributions
- Adjusting investment strategies
- Reducing unnecessary expenses
- Seeking additional income sources

Step 6: Monitor and Adjust

Regularly review your financial plan to ensure you're on track. Life circumstances and economic conditions may change, necessitating adjustments to your strategies.

Embracing Proactive Financial Planning

The Benefits of Early and Continuous Planning

While some may feel it's too late to start planning, proactive financial planning can yield significant benefits regardless of when you begin.

1. Maximizing Existing Resources

Even with limited savings, strategic planning can help you make the most of the resources you have. This includes optimizing Social Security benefits, leveraging pensions, and making informed investment choices.

2. Minimizing Risks

Proactive planning helps identify potential risks and develop strategies to mitigate them. This includes diversifying investments, securing adequate insurance, and planning for healthcare needs.

3. Enhancing Flexibility

A well-crafted financial plan provides the flexibility to adapt to changing circumstances, such as unexpected expenses or shifts in income sources.

Building a Support System

Surrounding yourself with a support system can enhance your financial planning efforts.

1. Professional Advisors

Engage with financial advisors, accountants, and legal professionals who can offer expert guidance tailored to your needs.

2. Peer Support

Connect with peers who are also navigating retirement planning. Sharing experiences and advice can provide valuable insights and emotional support.

3. Family Involvement

Involving family members in your financial planning can ensure that everyone is on the same page and can contribute to achieving shared goals.

Emphasizing Continuous Education

Financial planning is not a one-time task but an ongoing process that benefits from continuous education and adaptation.

1. Stay Updated

Keep abreast of changes in financial regulations, tax laws, and retirement planning strategies to ensure your plan remains relevant and effective.

2. Invest in Learning

Attend workshops, seminars, and webinars focused on retirement planning and personal finance to enhance your knowledge and skills.

3. Adapt to Change

Be prepared to adjust your financial plan in response to life changes, such as health issues, changes in marital status, or shifts in financial goals.

Real-Life Success Stories: Overcoming Financial Challenges

Maria's Journey to Financial Stability

Maria, a 65-year-old retired teacher, found herself with limited savings and a modest pension. Initially, she felt overwhelmed by her financial situation. However, Maria decided to take proactive steps to improve her financial health.

- **Assessing Finances**: Maria conducted a thorough review of her assets and liabilities, identifying areas

where she could reduce expenses and increase savings.
- **Seeking Professional Help**: She consulted a financial advisor who helped her develop a diversified investment strategy tailored to her risk tolerance and retirement goals.
- **Maximizing Social Security**: Maria adjusted the timing of her Social Security benefits to maximize her monthly income, resulting in a higher lifetime payout.
- **Generating Additional Income**: She began tutoring students in her spare time, leveraging her teaching skills to create a supplementary income stream.
- **Result**: Through these proactive measures, Maria increased her retirement savings by 30% over five years and achieved greater financial stability and peace of mind.

Tom's Path to Debt-Free Retirement

Tom, a 62-year-old engineer, was burdened with significant mortgage and credit card debt as he approached retirement. Determined to enter retirement debt-free, Tom took the following steps:

- **Debt Consolidation**: Tom consolidated his high-interest credit card debt into a lower-interest personal loan, reducing his monthly payments.
- **Budget Overhaul**: He created a strict budget, cutting discretionary spending and redirecting those funds toward debt repayment.
- **Home Equity Utilization**: Tom tapped into his home equity to pay off his mortgage, eliminating a major monthly expense and freeing up resources for savings and investments.

- **Result**: Within three years, Tom became entirely debt-free, significantly improving his financial outlook and enabling him to enjoy a more comfortable retirement.

Linda's Strategic Investment Approach

Linda, a 68-year-old entrepreneur, had accumulated modest savings but wanted to ensure her funds would sustain her throughout her retirement years.

- **Diversified Portfolio**: Linda worked with her financial advisor to diversify her investment portfolio, balancing growth-oriented stocks with stable bonds and income-generating real estate investments.
- **Regular Portfolio Reviews**: She scheduled annual reviews of her investment strategy to adjust her asset allocation based on market conditions and her evolving financial needs.
- **Tax-Efficient Investing**: Linda implemented tax-efficient investment strategies, such as utilizing tax-advantaged accounts and harvesting tax losses, to maximize her after-tax returns.
- **Result**: Linda's strategic approach to investing resulted in a robust and resilient portfolio that provided a steady income stream and preserved her capital, ensuring financial security throughout her retirement.

Embracing the Journey Ahead

Facing financial facts without fear is not about dwelling on the challenges but about empowering yourself to take control of your financial future. By assessing your current situation honestly, building your financial literacy, and embracing proactive planning, you can navigate the complexities of retirement with confidence and resilience.

Taking the First Step

The journey toward financial security begins with a single step—acknowledging where you are and envisioning where you want to be. Here's how to get started:

1. **Set Aside Time for Reflection**: Dedicate specific times to review your finances without distractions. This focused effort can provide clarity and direction.
2. **Seek Professional Guidance**: If you're unsure where to begin, consulting with a financial advisor can offer personalized insights and strategies.
3. **Educate Yourself**: Invest time in learning about personal finance, retirement planning, and investment strategies. Knowledge is a powerful tool in achieving financial independence.
4. **Create a Vision Board**: Visualize your retirement goals by creating a vision board. This can serve as a daily reminder of your aspirations and motivate you to stay on track.

Building Momentum

Once you've taken the initial steps, maintaining momentum is key to achieving your financial goals.

1. Celebrate Small Wins

Acknowledge and celebrate each milestone you reach, whether it's paying off a debt, increasing your savings, or successfully sticking to your budget. These small victories build confidence and encourage continued progress.

2. Stay Flexible

Life is unpredictable, and so is the financial landscape. Stay flexible and be prepared to adjust your plans as needed to accommodate changes in your personal circumstances or the broader economy.

3. Keep the End Goal in Sight

Regularly remind yourself of your long-term financial goals. Whether it's traveling the world, supporting your grandchildren's education, or leaving a legacy, keeping your objectives in mind can help you stay motivated and focused.

The Path Forward

Facing financial facts without fear is a transformative process that can lead to greater financial security and peace of mind. By embracing honesty, education, and proactive planning, you can overcome financial challenges and create a retirement that is not only sustainable but also fulfilling and enjoyable.

Final Thoughts

Understanding and addressing your financial situation is a critical aspect of preparing for retirement. While the statistics may seem intimidating, remember that knowledge and proactive action can significantly alter your financial trajectory. By assessing your savings, confronting your financial realities with courage, and implementing a strategic plan, you can navigate the complexities of retirement with confidence and optimism.

As you move forward, keep in mind that financial planning is a continuous journey. Regularly revisiting your goals, adapting to new circumstances, and seeking out resources and support will ensure that you remain on a path toward financial freedom and a fulfilling retirement.

Reflective Questions

1. **What is my current financial situation?**

   Take a detailed look at your assets, liabilities, income, and expenses to understand where you stand financially.

2. **What are my short-term and long-term financial goals?**

   Define what you want to achieve in both the near and distant future to guide your financial planning efforts.

3. **What steps can I take today to improve my financial health?**

   Identify actionable measures you can implement immediately to start moving toward your financial goals.

4. **Who can support me in my financial planning journey?**

   Consider reaching out to financial advisors, trusted friends, or family members who can provide guidance and support.

5. **How can I continue to educate myself about personal finance and retirement planning?**

Explore resources such as books, online courses, and workshops to enhance your financial literacy and confidence.

Chapter 3: Triumphs After 60: Stories of Success

Inspiring Journeys to Financial Freedom

Turning 60 often signifies a milestone—a time to reflect on past achievements and look forward to the future with hope and ambition. For many, this period can also present financial challenges. However, as the stories in this chapter illustrate, it's never too late to take control of your finances and create a secure, fulfilling retirement. These inspiring anecdotes showcase individuals who have successfully navigated their financial journeys after 60, highlighting diverse paths to improvement and security.

Maria's Path to Financial Independence
Starting Fresh with Financial Literacy

Maria Rodriguez, a 63-year-old retired nurse, found herself facing unexpected financial difficulties after her pension was reduced due to hospital budget cuts. With limited savings and mounting medical expenses, Maria felt overwhelmed. Determined not to let her situation dictate her future, she decided to take proactive steps toward financial stability.

Steps Maria Took:

1. **Educating Herself:** Maria enrolled in free online courses about personal finance and investment. Understanding the basics of budgeting, saving, and investing empowered her to make informed decisions.

2. **Reducing Expenses:** She meticulously reviewed her monthly expenses, identifying areas where she could cut costs. By downsizing her living arrangements and eliminating unnecessary subscriptions, Maria managed to save an additional $500 each month.
3. **Generating Additional Income:** Leveraging her nursing background, Maria began offering private health consultations and wellness coaching. This not only supplemented her income but also allowed her to stay engaged and active.

Outcome:

Within two years, Maria had not only stabilized her finances but also built a modest investment portfolio. Her newfound financial literacy enabled her to navigate economic uncertainties with confidence, ensuring a secure and comfortable retirement.

Tom's Entrepreneurial Leap
From Engineer to Successful Business Owner

At 65, Tom Henderson, a retired mechanical engineer, faced the prospect of dipping into his savings earlier than planned due to rising healthcare costs. Rather than viewing this as a setback, Tom saw an opportunity to pursue a long-held passion for woodworking.

Steps Tom Took:

1. **Starting Small:** Tom began by creating handmade furniture pieces in his garage. He shared his creations on local community boards and at craft fairs, receiving positive feedback and growing interest.

2. **Building an Online Presence:** Recognizing the potential of online sales, Tom invested time in building a website and utilizing social media platforms to showcase his work. He also learned about e-commerce tools to streamline his sales process.
3. **Scaling Up:** As demand increased, Tom expanded his workshop, hired a few part-time helpers, and diversified his product line to include custom designs and home décor items.

Outcome:

Tom's woodworking business flourished, providing him with a steady income stream that far exceeded his initial projections. His entrepreneurial venture not only alleviated financial pressures but also brought immense personal satisfaction, proving that it's never too late to start a successful business.

Linda's Strategic Investment Approach

Maximizing Retirement Funds Through Smart Investments

Linda Thompson, a 68-year-old retired teacher, had diligently saved for retirement but was concerned about the sustainability of her savings in the face of market volatility and increasing expenses. Determined to protect and grow her nest egg, Linda sought professional financial advice.

Steps Linda Took:

1. **Consulting a Financial Advisor:** Linda partnered with a certified financial planner who helped her assess her risk tolerance and investment goals. Together, they developed a diversified investment strategy tailored to her needs.

2. **Diversifying Her Portfolio:** To mitigate risks, Linda diversified her investments across various asset classes, including stocks, bonds, real estate, and dividend-paying mutual funds. This balanced approach provided both growth potential and income stability.
3. **Regular Portfolio Reviews:** Linda committed to annual portfolio reviews with her advisor to adjust her investments based on market conditions and her evolving financial needs. This proactive management ensured her portfolio remained aligned with her retirement objectives.

Outcome:

Linda's strategic investment approach yielded impressive returns, significantly boosting her retirement funds. The diversified portfolio provided her with a reliable income stream and a safety net against market downturns, enhancing her financial security and peace of mind.

George's Debt-Free Retirement
Eliminating Debt to Enhance Financial Well-Being

George Martinez, a 61-year-old retired electrician, entered retirement with a significant amount of debt, including a mortgage and several credit card balances. Concerned about the financial strain, George resolved to eliminate his debts to achieve a debt-free retirement.

Steps George Took:

1. **Creating a Debt Repayment Plan:** George listed all his debts, prioritizing them by interest rate. He focused on paying off high-interest credit cards first

while making minimum payments on lower-interest debts.
2. **Increasing Income:** To accelerate debt repayment, George took on a part-time job as a handyman. The additional income was dedicated entirely to paying down his debts.
3. **Reducing Expenses:** George cut back on non-essential expenses, such as dining out and entertainment, reallocating those funds toward his debt repayment plan.

Outcome:

Within three years, George successfully eliminated all his debts, including his mortgage. Being debt-free provided him with greater financial flexibility and reduced stress, allowing him to enjoy his retirement without the burden of ongoing debt payments.

Emma's Journey to Financial Resilience
Leveraging Community Resources and Support

Emma Johnson, a 70-year-old retired librarian, faced financial challenges after her husband's passing, which left her without a stable income. Determined to rebuild her financial standing, Emma sought out community resources and support systems.

Steps Emma Took:

1. **Accessing Community Programs:** Emma discovered local non-profit organizations that offered financial counseling, meal programs, and assistance with utilities. These resources helped her reduce her monthly expenses and stabilize her finances.

2. **Joining Senior Networks:** By joining senior community groups and online forums, Emma connected with others facing similar financial challenges. These networks provided emotional support, practical advice, and opportunities for collaborative initiatives.
3. **Pursuing Volunteer Work:** Emma began volunteering at local libraries and community centers, which not only provided her with a sense of purpose but also led to paid opportunities and networking connections.

Outcome:

Emma's proactive approach and utilization of community resources significantly improved her financial situation. She gained access to essential services, built a supportive network, and discovered new income opportunities, enhancing her financial resilience and overall well-being.

Lessons from These Triumphs

The stories of Maria, Tom, Linda, George, and Emma highlight several key themes that can inspire and guide others seeking financial improvement after 60:

1. **Education and Financial Literacy:** Understanding personal finance and investment principles is crucial. Continuous learning empowers individuals to make informed decisions and take control of their financial futures.
2. **Entrepreneurial Spirit:** Pursuing passions and turning them into income-generating ventures can provide financial stability and personal fulfillment, regardless of age.
3. **Strategic Planning:** Developing a comprehensive financial plan, including diversification of

investments and proactive debt management, can enhance financial security and resilience.
4. **Utilizing Support Systems:** Accessing community resources, seeking professional advice, and building supportive networks are essential components of successful financial planning.
5. **Resilience and Adaptability:** Facing financial challenges with determination and flexibility allows individuals to overcome obstacles and achieve their goals.

It's Never Too Late to Make a Positive Change

These triumphs demonstrate that no matter your age, you have the power to reshape your financial future. Whether it's through education, entrepreneurship, strategic investing, debt elimination, or leveraging community support, there are multiple paths to financial improvement and security.

Takeaway Points:

- **Assess Your Situation:** Start by understanding your current financial standing. Identify your assets, liabilities, income sources, and expenses.
- **Set Clear Goals:** Define what financial success looks like for you. Whether it's eliminating debt, increasing savings, or starting a business, clear goals provide direction and motivation.
- **Seek Knowledge and Support:** Educate yourself about personal finance and seek advice from professionals and supportive communities.
- **Take Action:** Implement your financial plan with determination and adaptability. Celebrate your progress and stay committed to your goals.

Final Thought:

Your journey to financial freedom after 60 is uniquely yours. Let these stories inspire you to take the first step, explore diverse strategies, and embrace the possibilities that lie ahead. Remember, it's never too late to make a positive change and achieve the financial security and peace of mind you deserve.

Reflective Questions:

1. **Which of these stories resonates most with your current financial situation, and why?**
2. **What steps can you take today to start your own journey toward financial improvement?**
3. **Who in your network can support you in achieving your financial goals?**
4. **What passions or skills can you leverage to generate additional income?**
5. **How can you utilize community resources to enhance your financial well-being?**

Chapter 4: Supercharging Your Savings: Proven Techniques

Unlocking the Potential of Your Retirement Funds

Reaching retirement is a significant milestone, but ensuring that your savings are sufficient to support the lifestyle you desire requires thoughtful planning and strategic action. This chapter provides actionable strategies to boost your retirement funds, covering smart investments, effective budgeting, and diligent debt management. Tailored specifically for those over 60, these step-by-step guidelines will help you maximize your financial resources and achieve a secure, fulfilling retirement.

1. Smart Investments: Making Your Money Work for You

Investing wisely is crucial to growing your retirement funds. While the approach may differ from pre-retirement investing, there are several strategies that can help you enhance your portfolio's performance while managing risk.

a. Diversify Your Portfolio

Why It Matters: Diversification reduces risk by spreading investments across various asset classes, such as stocks, bonds, real estate, and mutual funds. This approach minimizes the impact of poor performance in any single investment.

How to Do It:

- **Assess Your Current Investments:** Review your existing portfolio to identify areas of concentration.
- **Spread Your Investments:** Allocate funds across different sectors and asset types. For example, balance growth-oriented stocks with stable bonds.
- **Include Alternative Investments:** Consider adding real estate or dividend-paying stocks to generate additional income streams.

b. Focus on Dividend-Paying Stocks

Why It Matters: Dividend-paying stocks provide regular income, which can supplement your retirement funds. They also tend to be less volatile than growth stocks.

How to Do It:

- **Research Reliable Companies:** Look for companies with a history of consistent dividend payments.
- **Reinvest Dividends:** Consider reinvesting dividends to compound your returns over time.
- **Monitor Performance:** Regularly review the performance of your dividend stocks to ensure they continue to meet your income needs.

c. Utilize Low-Cost Index Funds and ETFs

Why It Matters: Index funds and Exchange-Traded Funds (ETFs) offer broad market exposure with lower fees compared to actively managed funds, enhancing your net returns.

How to Do It:

- **Choose Broad Market Indexes:** Invest in funds that track major indexes like the S&P 500 or Total Market Index.
- **Minimize Fees:** Select funds with low expense ratios to maximize your investment growth.
- **Automate Investments:** Set up automatic contributions to consistently build your investment portfolio.

d. Consider Annuities for Guaranteed Income

Why It Matters: Annuities can provide a steady income stream, ensuring financial stability throughout retirement.

How to Do It:

- **Understand the Types:** Explore different annuity options, such as fixed, variable, and immediate annuities.
- **Evaluate Costs and Benefits:** Assess fees, payout options, and the financial strength of the insurance company offering the annuity.
- **Integrate with Your Portfolio:** Use annuities as part of a diversified income strategy to balance other investments.

2. Effective Budgeting: Maximizing Every Dollar

Creating and maintaining a budget is fundamental to managing your retirement funds effectively. A well-structured budget helps you control expenses, increase savings, and avoid unnecessary debt.

a. Track Your Spending

Why It Matters: Understanding where your money goes is the first step in identifying areas for improvement.

How to Do It:

- **Use Budgeting Tools:** Utilize apps like Mint, YNAB (You Need A Budget), or Personal Capital to monitor your spending habits.
- **Categorize Expenses:** Break down your expenses into categories such as housing, utilities, food, healthcare, and entertainment.
- **Identify Patterns:** Look for recurring expenses and assess whether they align with your financial goals.

b. Create a Realistic Budget

Why It Matters: A practical budget ensures that your spending aligns with your income and savings objectives.

How to Do It:

- **Set Spending Limits:** Allocate specific amounts to each expense category based on your tracked spending.
- **Prioritize Needs Over Wants:** Focus on essential expenses first, then allocate funds for discretionary spending.
- **Include Savings Goals:** Treat savings as a mandatory expense, ensuring you consistently contribute to your retirement funds.

c. Reduce Unnecessary Expenses

Why It Matters: Cutting back on non-essential spending can free up funds to bolster your savings and investments.

How to Do It:

- **Evaluate Subscriptions:** Cancel services and memberships you no longer use or need.
- **Opt for Cost-Effective Alternatives:** Choose generic brands, cook at home instead of dining out, and find free or low-cost entertainment options.
- **Implement Energy-Saving Measures:** Reduce utility bills by adopting energy-efficient practices and appliances.

d. Plan for Major Expenses

Why It Matters: Anticipating significant costs helps prevent financial strain and ensures you have the necessary funds when needed.

How to Do It:

- **Create an Emergency Fund:** Save three to six months' worth of living expenses to cover unexpected events.
- **Budget for Healthcare:** Allocate funds for medical expenses, including insurance premiums, medications, and potential long-term care.
- **Plan for Home Maintenance:** Set aside money for home repairs and improvements to avoid costly last-minute expenses.

3. Debt Management: Eliminating Financial Burdens

Managing and eliminating debt is essential for maximizing your retirement savings and reducing financial stress.

a. Assess Your Debt Situation

Why It Matters: Understanding the extent of your debt helps you develop an effective repayment strategy.

How to Do It:

- **List All Debts:** Include mortgages, car loans, credit card balances, and any other outstanding debts.
- **Calculate Interest Rates:** Identify which debts carry the highest interest rates to prioritize repayment.
- **Evaluate Monthly Payments:** Determine how much you're paying toward each debt monthly.

b. Develop a Debt Repayment Plan

Why It Matters: A structured plan provides a clear path to eliminating debt and freeing up funds for savings.

How to Do It:

- **Choose a Repayment Strategy:** Consider methods like the Debt Snowball (paying off smallest debts first) or Debt Avalanche (tackling highest-interest debts first).
- **Set Clear Goals:** Define specific milestones, such as paying off a certain debt within six months.
- **Automate Payments:** Set up automatic payments to ensure consistency and avoid missed deadlines.

c. Consolidate and Refinance

Why It Matters: Consolidating or refinancing debt can lower interest rates and simplify repayment.

How to Do It:

- **Explore Consolidation Loans:** Combine multiple debts into a single loan with a lower interest rate.
- **Refinance High-Interest Loans:** Refinance mortgages or car loans to take advantage of lower interest rates.

- **Assess Fees and Terms:** Ensure that the benefits of consolidation or refinancing outweigh any associated costs.

d. Avoid Accumulating New Debt

Why It Matters: Preventing new debt is crucial for maintaining financial stability and focusing on repayment.

How to Do It:

- **Use Cash or Debit:** Limit the use of credit cards by paying with cash or debit to stay within your budget.
- **Build an Emergency Fund:** Having savings for unexpected expenses reduces the need to rely on credit.
- **Monitor Credit Reports:** Regularly check your credit reports to stay aware of your financial standing and identify potential issues early.

4. Step-by-Step Guidance for Boosting Your Savings

Implementing these strategies requires a systematic approach. Follow these steps to supercharge your savings and enhance your financial security.

Step 1: Conduct a Financial Assessment

Why It Matters: A comprehensive understanding of your current financial situation is the foundation for effective planning.

How to Do It:

- **Calculate Net Worth:** Subtract your total liabilities from your total assets to determine your net worth.

- **Review Income Sources:** Identify all sources of income, including Social Security, pensions, investments, and part-time work.
- **Analyze Expenses:** Track your spending to understand where your money goes each month.

Step 2: Set Clear Financial Goals

Why It Matters: Defining your objectives provides direction and motivation for your financial efforts.

How to Do It:

- **Short-Term Goals:** Examples include paying off credit card debt, building an emergency fund, or saving for a vacation.
- **Long-Term Goals:** These might involve ensuring a comfortable retirement, leaving a legacy, or supporting family members.
- **Prioritize Goals:** Rank your goals based on importance and urgency to focus your efforts effectively.

Step 3: Create and Implement a Budget

Why It Matters: A budget helps you control your finances, reduce unnecessary expenses, and increase savings.

How to Do It:

- **Allocate Funds:** Assign specific amounts to each expense category based on your financial assessment.
- **Monitor Progress:** Regularly review your spending against your budget to ensure you're staying on track.
- **Adjust as Needed:** Be flexible and adjust your budget to accommodate changes in income or expenses.

Step 4: Optimize Your Investments

Why It Matters: Maximizing the performance of your investments can significantly boost your retirement funds.

How to Do It:

- **Review Your Portfolio:** Assess the performance and diversification of your current investments.
- **Adjust Allocation:** Rebalance your portfolio to maintain an appropriate mix of asset classes based on your risk tolerance and goals.
- **Seek Professional Advice:** Consult with a financial advisor to refine your investment strategy and explore new opportunities.

Step 5: Manage and Eliminate Debt

Why It Matters: Reducing debt frees up more of your income for savings and investments.

How to Do It:

- **Prioritize High-Interest Debt:** Focus on paying off debts with the highest interest rates first.
- **Implement a Repayment Plan:** Follow a structured strategy, such as the Debt Avalanche or Debt Snowball method.
- **Avoid New Debt:** Stick to your budget and use cash or debit to prevent accumulating additional debt.

Step 6: Increase Income Streams

Why It Matters: Additional income can accelerate your savings growth and provide financial flexibility.

How to Do It:

- **Part-Time Work:** Consider part-time employment in a field you enjoy or have expertise in.
- **Freelancing or Consulting:** Leverage your professional skills to offer services on a freelance basis.
- **Monetize Hobbies:** Turn hobbies or passions into income-generating activities, such as crafting, writing, or gardening.

Step 7: Leverage Technology and Resources

Why It Matters: Utilizing financial tools and resources can simplify money management and enhance your financial planning.

How to Do It:

- **Budgeting Apps:** Use apps like Mint or YNAB to track expenses and manage your budget efficiently.
- **Investment Platforms:** Explore robo-advisors or online brokerage accounts to manage your investments with ease.
- **Educational Resources:** Continuously educate yourself through books, webinars, and workshops focused on personal finance and retirement planning.

5. Tailoring Strategies for Those Over 60

Age-specific considerations are essential for effective financial planning. Here are tailored strategies to address the unique needs of individuals over 60.

a. Prioritize Stability and Security

Why It Matters: As retirement nears or begins, preserving your capital becomes more important to ensure long-term financial security.

How to Do It:

- **Shift to Conservative Investments:** Allocate more of your portfolio to bonds, dividend-paying stocks, and other low-risk investments.
- **Maintain Liquidity:** Keep a portion of your savings in easily accessible accounts to cover immediate expenses without needing to liquidate investments.

b. Maximize Social Security Benefits

Why It Matters: Social Security is a significant source of income for many retirees. Optimizing your benefits can enhance your overall financial situation.

How to Do It:

- **Delay Benefits:** Consider delaying the start of Social Security benefits beyond your full retirement age to increase your monthly payments.
- **Coordinate with Spousal Benefits:** If married, strategize with your spouse to maximize combined benefits, potentially increasing total household income.

c. Plan for Healthcare Expenses

Why It Matters: Healthcare costs can be a substantial burden in retirement. Proactively planning for these expenses ensures you're prepared for medical needs.

How to Do It:

- **Understand Medicare:** Familiarize yourself with Medicare options and consider supplemental insurance to cover gaps.

- **Save for Medical Costs:** Allocate part of your savings specifically for healthcare expenses, including out-of-pocket costs and long-term care needs.

d. Consider Downsizing

Why It Matters: Reducing your living expenses by downsizing can free up funds for savings, investments, or other financial goals.

How to Do It:

- **Evaluate Your Needs:** Assess whether your current home meets your needs or if a smaller, more manageable space would be more cost-effective.
- **Sell and Relocate:** If downsizing, sell your current home and relocate to a more affordable area, using the proceeds to enhance your financial position.

e. Stay Engaged and Informed

Why It Matters: Staying active and informed helps you adapt to changing financial landscapes and seize new opportunities.

How to Do It:

- **Join Financial Workshops:** Participate in workshops and seminars focused on retirement planning and investment strategies.
- **Engage with Communities:** Connect with other retirees through clubs, online forums, or local organizations to share experiences and advice.

Empowering Your Financial Future

Supercharging your savings in retirement is a multifaceted endeavor that involves smart investing, effective budgeting, and diligent debt management. By implementing the strategies outlined in this chapter, you can enhance your financial security and enjoy a more comfortable and fulfilling retirement.

Key Takeaways:

- **Diversify Investments:** Spread your investments across various asset classes to minimize risk and maximize returns.
- **Create a Realistic Budget:** Control your spending, prioritize essential expenses, and allocate funds for savings.
- **Manage and Eliminate Debt:** Develop a structured repayment plan and avoid accumulating new debt.
- **Increase Income Streams:** Explore part-time work, freelancing, or monetizing hobbies to boost your income.
- **Tailor Strategies for Your Age:** Focus on stability, maximize Social Security benefits, plan for healthcare costs, consider downsizing, and stay engaged with financial education.

Action Steps:

1. **Assess Your Financial Situation:** Conduct a thorough review of your assets, liabilities, income, and expenses.
2. **Set Clear Goals:** Define what you want to achieve financially in retirement.
3. **Implement Strategies:** Start applying the investment, budgeting, and debt management techniques discussed.

4. **Seek Professional Advice:** Consult with a financial advisor to refine your strategies and ensure they align with your goals.
5. **Stay Committed:** Regularly review and adjust your financial plan to stay on track toward a secure and prosperous retirement.

By taking proactive steps today, you can supercharge your savings and build a robust financial foundation that supports your retirement dreams. Remember, it's never too late to make positive changes and secure the financial future you deserve.

Reflective Questions:

1. **Which investment strategies resonate most with your financial goals, and how can you implement them?**
2. **What areas of your budget can be adjusted to increase your savings?**
3. **How can you effectively manage or eliminate existing debt to enhance your financial stability?**
4. **What additional income streams can you explore to supplement your retirement funds?**
5. **How can you tailor these strategies to better fit your unique financial situation and retirement aspirations?**

Chapter 5: Unlocking the Full Potential of Social Security and Medicare

Maximizing Your Benefits for a Secure Retirement

Navigating the intricate landscapes of Social Security and Medicare is crucial for ensuring a comfortable and secure retirement. These programs form the backbone of financial and healthcare support for millions of Americans over 60. However, understanding how to maximize these benefits requires careful planning and informed decision-making. This chapter delves into strategies for optimizing your Social Security benefits, demystifying Medicare complexities, and providing actionable tips on timing and coordination to achieve the best possible outcomes.

1. Maximizing Social Security Benefits

Social Security is often a primary source of income for retirees, but many are unaware of how to fully leverage this program to enhance their financial security. Understanding the nuances of Social Security can significantly impact your retirement income.

a. Understanding Your Social Security Benefits

Before you can maximize your Social Security benefits, it's essential to understand how the program works:

- **Earnings Record**: Your Social Security benefits are based on your highest 35 years of earnings. Ensuring that you have a robust earnings record can maximize your benefits.

- **Full Retirement Age (FRA)**: FRA varies depending on your birth year, typically ranging from 66 to 67. Knowing your FRA is crucial for deciding when to start taking benefits.
- **Benefit Calculation**: Benefits are calculated using a formula that considers your average indexed monthly earnings (AIME) and your primary insurance amount (PIA).

b. Strategies to Maximize Benefits

1. Delay Claiming Benefits

One of the most effective ways to increase your Social Security benefits is by delaying the start of your benefits:

- **Delayed Retirement Credits (DRCs)**: For each year you delay claiming benefits past your FRA up to age 70, your benefits increase by a certain percentage (typically 8% per year). This can result in a significantly higher monthly benefit.
- **Longevity Consideration**: If you expect to live well into your 80s or beyond, delaying benefits can provide a higher lifetime payout.

Example: If your FRA is 66 and you choose to wait until 70 to claim benefits, you could receive approximately 32% more each month compared to claiming at FRA.

2. Coordinate Benefits with Your Spouse

For married couples, coordinating Social Security benefits can optimize total household income:

- **Spousal Benefits**: A spouse can receive up to 50% of the other spouse's FRA benefit if they claim at their FRA. This can be beneficial if one spouse has significantly higher earnings.

- **Survivor Benefits**: Upon the death of a spouse, the surviving spouse can claim the higher of their own benefit or the deceased spouse's benefit. Delaying the higher-earning spouse's benefits can increase survivor benefits.

Strategy:

- **Higher-Earning Spouse**: Delay claiming until age 70 to maximize DRCs.
- **Lower-Earning Spouse**: Claim spousal benefits at FRA to start receiving income earlier.

3. Optimize Tax Implications

Social Security benefits may be subject to federal income taxes depending on your total income:

- **Provisional Income**: This includes your adjusted gross income, nontaxable interest, and half of your Social Security benefits. If your provisional income exceeds certain thresholds, up to 85% of your benefits may be taxable.
- **Tax Planning**: Strategically managing other sources of income, such as retirement account withdrawals, can minimize the taxation of your Social Security benefits.

Tip: Work with a tax advisor to develop a withdrawal strategy that reduces your taxable income and maximizes your Social Security benefits.

c. Work Longer if Possible

Continuing to work while claiming Social Security benefits can have multiple advantages:

- **Increase Earnings Record**: Additional years of employment can replace lower-earning years, increasing your average indexed monthly earnings and, consequently, your benefits.
- **Earn Delayed Retirement Credits**: Working beyond FRA can allow you to delay claiming benefits, thus earning more DRCs.

Consideration: Ensure that working does not push you into higher tax brackets that could negate the benefits of increased Social Security income.

2. Navigating the Complexities of Medicare

Medicare is a vital program that provides health insurance to those over 65, but its complexities can be daunting. Understanding how to navigate Medicare effectively is essential for securing comprehensive health coverage without unnecessary costs.

a. Understanding Medicare Parts

Medicare is divided into several parts, each covering different aspects of healthcare:

- **Part A (Hospital Insurance)**: Covers inpatient hospital stays, skilled nursing facility care, hospice care, and some home health care. Most people do not pay a premium for Part A if they have paid Medicare taxes while working.
- **Part B (Medical Insurance)**: Covers certain doctors' services, outpatient care, medical supplies, and preventive services. Part B requires a monthly premium.
- **Part C (Medicare Advantage)**: An alternative to Original Medicare, offered by private companies.

These plans often include Part D and may offer additional benefits like dental and vision coverage.
- **Part D (Prescription Drug Coverage)**: Helps cover the cost of prescription drugs. Available as standalone plans or included in Medicare Advantage plans.

b. Enrolling in Medicare

Timely enrollment in Medicare is crucial to avoid penalties and ensure continuous coverage:

- **Initial Enrollment Period (IEP)**: Begins three months before the month you turn 65 and ends three months after the month you turn 65. Enrolling during this period avoids late enrollment penalties.
- **General Enrollment Period (GEP)**: Runs from January 1 to March 31 each year. Benefits start July 1 of the same year. Late enrollment penalties apply if you miss your IEP.
- **Special Enrollment Period (SEP)**: Available if you are still working and covered by an employer's health plan when you turn 65. You can enroll in Medicare without penalties during this period.

Tip: Coordinate your Medicare enrollment with your employer's health coverage to avoid gaps and penalties.

c. Choosing the Right Medicare Plan

Selecting the appropriate Medicare plan involves evaluating your healthcare needs and financial situation:

1. Original Medicare vs. Medicare Advantage

- **Original Medicare (Part A and Part B)**: Offers flexibility in choosing healthcare providers but does

not include prescription drug coverage (requires separate Part D).
- **Medicare Advantage (Part C)**: Provides an all-in-one alternative, often including Part D and additional benefits. These plans may have network restrictions and require referrals for specialists.

Consideration: If you prefer flexibility in choosing providers and want to add prescription drug coverage separately, Original Medicare may be suitable. If you prefer comprehensive coverage with additional benefits and are comfortable with network restrictions, Medicare Advantage could be a better choice.

2. Prescription Drug Plans (Part D)

- **Standalone Plans**: Can be added to Original Medicare to cover prescription medications.
- **Included in Medicare Advantage**: Many Medicare Advantage plans include Part D coverage.

Tip: Compare formularies (lists of covered drugs) and premiums to find a plan that best meets your medication needs.

3. Supplemental Insurance (Medigap)

- **What It Covers**: Medigap policies help cover out-of-pocket costs not covered by Original Medicare, such as copayments, coinsurance, and deductibles.
- **Standardized Plans**: Available in various standardized plans (A through N), each offering different levels of coverage.

Consideration: If you choose Original Medicare, a Medigap policy can provide additional financial protection against unexpected healthcare costs.

d. Understanding Medicare Costs

Managing the costs associated with Medicare is essential for maintaining financial stability:

- **Premiums**: Part B and Part D plans require monthly premiums. These can vary based on income and plan choices.
- **Deductibles and Coinsurance**: Be aware of out-of-pocket costs associated with each Medicare part. Medigap policies can help mitigate these expenses.
- **Late Enrollment Penalties**: Delaying enrollment in Part B or Part D without having creditable coverage can result in higher premiums for life.

Tip: Factor in all potential costs when selecting a Medicare plan to ensure it fits within your budget.

3. Timing and Coordination for Optimal Results

Strategic timing and coordination of Social Security and Medicare benefits can enhance your overall retirement plan, maximizing income and minimizing costs.

a. Coordinating Social Security and Medicare Enrollment

Aligning your Social Security and Medicare enrollment is crucial to avoid penalties and ensure seamless coverage:

- **IEP Coordination**: Enroll in Medicare during your Initial Enrollment Period when you start receiving Social Security benefits.
- **SEP for Medicare**: If you delay Social Security benefits and continue working, you can enroll in Medicare during a Special Enrollment Period, ensuring you don't face late enrollment penalties.

Strategy: If you plan to continue working past 65 and are covered by an employer's health plan, delay Medicare enrollment until your SEP becomes active, allowing you to coordinate the timing with your Social Security benefits.

b. Strategic Claiming of Social Security Benefits

Deciding when to claim Social Security benefits affects both the amount you receive and your Medicare coverage:

- **Claiming at FRA**: Start receiving benefits at your Full Retirement Age for a balanced approach between benefit amount and duration.
- **Delaying Benefits**: Postponing benefits beyond FRA increases your monthly payout through DRCs, which can be advantageous if you have a longer life expectancy.
- **Early Claiming**: Claiming before FRA results in reduced monthly benefits but allows for earlier access to funds.

Tip: Consider your health, financial needs, and life expectancy when deciding the optimal time to claim Social Security benefits.

c. Maximizing Lifetime Benefits

To maximize your lifetime benefits, consider how Social Security and Medicare interact over your retirement years:

- **Spousal Coordination**: For married couples, coordinate benefits to maximize household income. One spouse can delay benefits to increase survivor benefits, while the other can claim earlier.
- **Health and Longevity**: If you expect to live a long life, delaying Social Security can provide higher

lifetime benefits, which can be complemented by stable Medicare coverage.
- **Income Management**: Use Social Security as part of a broader income strategy, supplementing it with investments and other income sources to maintain financial flexibility.

d. Leveraging Professional Advice

Navigating the timing and coordination of Social Security and Medicare can be complex. Seeking professional advice can help you make informed decisions:

- **Financial Advisors**: Certified financial planners can help integrate Social Security and Medicare into your overall retirement strategy.
- **Social Security Experts**: Consultants specializing in Social Security can provide personalized guidance on optimizing your benefits.
- **Medicare Counselors**: Certified Medicare counselors can assist in selecting the right Medicare plans and understanding coverage options.

Tip: Invest in a consultation with a financial advisor who understands both Social Security and Medicare to develop a cohesive retirement plan.

4. Practical Steps to Unlock the Full Potential

Implementing the strategies discussed requires a systematic approach. Follow these practical steps to maximize your Social Security and Medicare benefits effectively.

Step 1: Assess Your Current Situation

- **Review Earnings Record**: Ensure your Social Security statement accurately reflects your earnings history. Discrepancies can affect your benefits.
- **Understand Medicare Options**: Familiarize yourself with the different parts of Medicare and how they fit into your healthcare needs.

Step 2: Develop a Comprehensive Plan

- **Set Clear Objectives**: Define what you aim to achieve with your Social Security and Medicare benefits, such as maximizing income or securing comprehensive health coverage.
- **Create a Timeline**: Establish a timeline for when to enroll in Medicare and when to start claiming Social Security benefits based on your financial goals and health considerations.

Step 3: Enroll in Medicare on Time

- **Initial Enrollment Period**: Ensure you enroll in Medicare during your IEP to avoid late enrollment penalties.
- **Review and Select Plans**: Compare Original Medicare, Medicare Advantage, Part D plans, and Medigap policies to choose the coverage that best suits your needs.

Step 4: Optimize Social Security Claiming Strategy

- **Determine FRA**: Know your Full Retirement Age and use it as a benchmark for your claiming strategy.

- **Consider Delaying Benefits**: If feasible, delay claiming benefits to earn DRCs and increase your monthly payout.
- **Coordinate with Spouse**: Develop a joint strategy with your spouse to maximize combined benefits and survivor payouts.

Step 5: Integrate Social Security and Medicare into Your Financial Plan

- **Income Stream Planning**: Incorporate Social Security benefits into your overall income plan, balancing them with other income sources such as pensions, investments, and part-time work.
- **Healthcare Cost Management**: Align your Medicare choices with your healthcare needs to minimize out-of-pocket costs and ensure comprehensive coverage.

Step 6: Regularly Review and Adjust Your Strategy

- **Annual Reviews**: Conduct yearly reviews of your Social Security and Medicare plans to ensure they continue to meet your needs and adjust for any changes in your circumstances.
- **Stay Informed**: Keep abreast of any changes in Social Security and Medicare regulations that could impact your benefits.

Tip: Schedule regular check-ins with your financial advisor to stay on track and make necessary adjustments to your plan.

5. Overcoming Common Challenges

Maximizing Social Security and Medicare benefits isn't without its challenges. Understanding and addressing these common obstacles can help you navigate the process more smoothly.

a. Navigating Complex Regulations

The rules governing Social Security and Medicare are intricate and subject to change:

- **Stay Informed**: Regularly consult official resources such as the Social Security Administration (SSA) and Medicare websites for updates.
- **Seek Professional Help**: Utilize the expertise of financial advisors and Medicare counselors to interpret complex regulations and apply them to your situation.

b. Managing Health-Related Issues

Health issues can complicate your Social Security and Medicare planning:

- **Early Planning**: Anticipate potential health changes and plan your Medicare coverage accordingly, considering supplemental insurance if necessary.
- **Long-Term Care Considerations**: Explore options for long-term care insurance or savings strategies to cover future healthcare needs not covered by Medicare.

c. Avoiding Common Pitfalls

Many retirees fall into traps that can reduce their benefits or increase costs:

- **Avoid Early Claiming Penalties**: Understand the implications of claiming Social Security benefits before FRA and plan accordingly.
- **Prevent Coverage Gaps**: Ensure continuous Medicare coverage, especially if transitioning from employer-sponsored insurance.
- **Minimize Taxes**: Strategize your income sources to keep your Social Security benefits as tax-efficient as possible.

Tip: Create a checklist of key actions and milestones to ensure you don't overlook critical steps in your Social Security and Medicare planning.

6. Case Studies: Real-Life Examples

To illustrate the principles discussed, let's explore real-life scenarios where individuals successfully maximized their Social Security and Medicare benefits.

Case Study 1: Sarah's Strategic Delaying of Benefits

Background: Sarah, age 68, decided to delay claiming Social Security benefits until age 70 to maximize her monthly payout.

Strategy:

- **Delayed Retirement Credits**: By waiting three years beyond her FRA, Sarah earned DRCs, increasing her monthly benefits by 24%.

- **Investment Growth**: The additional income from delayed benefits allowed Sarah to invest more in a diversified portfolio, further enhancing her financial security.

Outcome: Sarah enjoys a higher monthly Social Security benefit, providing greater financial stability and flexibility in her retirement years.

Case Study 2: John's Comprehensive Medicare Plan

Background: John, age 66, opted for Original Medicare with a Medigap policy and a standalone Part D plan to cover his healthcare needs.

Strategy:

- **Medigap Coverage**: John's Medigap policy covers out-of-pocket costs, reducing his healthcare expenses significantly.
- **Part D Enrollment**: His standalone Part D plan ensures that his prescription drug costs are managed effectively.

Outcome: John experiences minimal out-of-pocket healthcare expenses, allowing him to allocate more funds toward savings and other retirement goals.

Case Study 3: Emily and Michael's Spousal Coordination

Background: Emily (age 64) and Michael (age 67) coordinated their Social Security benefits to maximize their household income.

Strategy:

- **Emily Claims Early**: Emily starts her benefits at 64, receiving a reduced monthly payout.
- **Michael Delays Benefits**: Michael waits until 70 to claim his benefits, significantly increasing his monthly payout.

Outcome: The combination of Emily's early benefits and Michael's delayed benefits provides a higher total household income than if both had claimed at FRA.

7. Additional Tips for Optimal Results

Beyond the primary strategies, several additional tips can help you unlock the full potential of Social Security and Medicare:

a. Utilize Online Tools and Resources

- **Social Security Calculators**: Use tools like the SSA's Retirement Estimator to project your benefits based on different claiming ages.
- **Medicare Plan Finders**: Explore Medicare's official website to compare plans, check coverage, and estimate costs.

b. Stay Proactive with Communication

- **Regularly Contact SSA and Medicare**: Maintain communication with the Social Security Administration and Medicare to stay updated on your benefits and any changes in regulations.
- **Document Everything**: Keep thorough records of your correspondence, applications, and benefits to avoid any discrepancies or issues.

c. Consider Professional Advocacy

- **Hire a Medicare Advocate**: If navigating Medicare feels overwhelming, consider hiring a Medicare advocate to assist with plan selection and enrollment.
- **Engage a Social Security Attorney**: For complex cases, such as disputes over benefits or late claims, a Social Security attorney can provide legal assistance.

d. Plan for the Unexpected

- **Emergency Funds**: Maintain an emergency fund to cover unexpected healthcare costs or delays in benefit claims.
- **Flexible Financial Planning**: Be prepared to adjust your plans in response to changes in your health, financial situation, or legislative updates affecting Social Security and Medicare.

8. Empowering Your Retirement with Knowledge and Strategy

Maximizing Social Security and Medicare benefits is a pivotal aspect of securing a comfortable and financially stable retirement. By understanding the intricacies of these programs, implementing strategic timing and coordination, and leveraging professional advice, you can unlock the full potential of your benefits.

Remember, every individual's situation is unique, and what works for one person may not be ideal for another. Therefore, personalized planning and continuous education are essential. Embrace the journey with confidence, knowing that with the right strategies, you can enhance your financial well-being and enjoy the retirement you deserve.

Key Takeaways:

- **Delayed Benefits Increase Payouts**: Waiting to claim Social Security beyond your FRA can significantly boost your monthly benefits.
- **Comprehensive Medicare Planning**: Understanding the different parts of Medicare and selecting the right combination of plans can minimize healthcare costs and ensure comprehensive coverage.
- **Strategic Coordination**: Aligning the timing of Social Security and Medicare enrollment with your financial goals and health needs can optimize your retirement income.
- **Professional Guidance**: Leveraging the expertise of financial advisors and Medicare counselors can help navigate complexities and tailor strategies to your unique situation.

Action Steps:

1. **Review Your Social Security Statement**: Ensure your earnings record is accurate and understand your projected benefits.
2. **Determine Your Optimal Claiming Age**: Assess whether delaying benefits aligns with your financial goals and health expectations.
3. **Evaluate Medicare Options**: Compare Original Medicare, Medicare Advantage, Part D, and Medigap policies to select the best coverage for your needs.

4. **Develop a Coordination Strategy**: Create a plan that synchronizes your Social Security and Medicare enrollment to maximize benefits and minimize costs.
5. **Consult Professionals**: Seek advice from financial advisors and Medicare experts to refine your strategies and stay informed about any changes in the programs.

Reflective Questions:

1. **When is the optimal time for me to claim my Social Security benefits, considering my health and financial needs?**
2. **Which Medicare plan combination best aligns with my healthcare requirements and budget?**
3. **How can I coordinate my Social Security and Medicare benefits to maximize household income and coverage?**
4. **What additional resources or professional advice can I seek to enhance my understanding and management of these programs?**
5. **How can I stay informed about changes in Social Security and Medicare regulations that may impact my benefits?**

Chapter 6: New Ventures: Earning Income on Your Terms

Embracing New Opportunities in Retirement

Retirement is not just an end but a new beginning—a time to explore fresh opportunities, pursue passions, and redefine what work means to you. Many individuals over 60 are discovering that their golden years can be a period of vibrant activity, financial growth, and personal fulfillment. This chapter delves into the possibilities of part-time work, entrepreneurial ventures, and turning hobbies into profitable endeavors, all while maintaining a harmonious balance between work and leisure.

1. Exploring Part-Time Work and Entrepreneurial Opportunities

a. The Appeal of Part-Time Work

Part-time work offers a flexible way to earn income without the demands of a full-time job. It allows retirees to stay active, engage with others, and contribute their skills and experience to the workforce.

Benefits of Part-Time Work:

- **Flexibility:** Choose hours that fit your lifestyle and other commitments.
- **Social Interaction:** Stay connected with colleagues and meet new people.
- **Skill Utilization:** Apply your professional skills in a less pressured environment.

- **Supplemental Income:** Enhance your financial security without the need for a demanding schedule.

Popular Part-Time Jobs for Seniors:

- **Consulting:** Leverage your expertise to advise businesses or individuals in your field.
- **Teaching or Tutoring:** Share your knowledge through educational roles, whether in schools, community centers, or online platforms.
- **Customer Service:** Engage with customers in retail, hospitality, or support roles.
- **Freelancing:** Offer services such as writing, graphic design, or bookkeeping on a freelance basis.

b. Entrepreneurial Opportunities

For those with a penchant for creativity and independence, entrepreneurship offers the chance to build something meaningful while generating income.

Types of Entrepreneurial Ventures:

- **Small Businesses:** Open a local shop, café, or service-based business that caters to your community.
- **Online Businesses:** Start an e-commerce store, offer digital products, or provide online consulting services.
- **Franchising:** Invest in a franchise that aligns with your interests and offers a proven business model.
- **Home-Based Businesses:** Run a business from the comfort of your home, such as crafting, baking, or virtual assistance.

Steps to Start an Entrepreneurial Venture:

1. **Identify Your Niche:** Determine what products or services you are passionate about and where there is market demand.
2. **Create a Business Plan:** Outline your business goals, target audience, financial projections, and marketing strategies.
3. **Secure Funding:** Explore funding options such as personal savings, loans, or small business grants.
4. **Launch and Market:** Develop a strong brand presence and utilize marketing channels like social media, local advertising, and word-of-mouth to attract customers.
5. **Scale Gradually:** Start small, learn from initial experiences, and expand your business as you gain confidence and resources.

Example:
John, a 65-year-old retired engineer, turned his passion for woodworking into a successful online store selling handcrafted furniture. By leveraging his technical skills and attention to detail, John created high-quality pieces that attracted customers worldwide. His business not only provided a steady income but also gave him immense personal satisfaction.

2. Turning Hobbies and Passions into Profitable Endeavors

a. Monetizing Your Passions

Retirement offers the perfect opportunity to turn hobbies and passions into income-generating activities. Whether it's gardening, painting, writing, or cooking, there are numerous ways to profit from what you love doing.

Steps to Monetize Your Hobbies:

1. **Assess Market Demand:** Research if there is a market for your hobby. Identify potential customers and understand their needs.
2. **Develop Your Product or Service:** Create high-quality products or services that showcase your expertise and passion.
3. **Create a Business Model:** Decide how you will sell your products or services—through online platforms, local markets, or direct sales.
4. **Promote Your Offerings:** Use social media, word-of-mouth, and local advertising to spread the word about your offerings.
5. **Build a Brand:** Establish a strong brand identity that reflects your passion and attracts your target audience.

Examples:

- **Crafting and Handmade Goods:** Sarah, an avid knitter, started selling her handmade scarves and blankets on Etsy. Her unique designs quickly gained popularity, allowing her to turn her knitting hobby into a profitable business.
- **Photography:** Mark, a photography enthusiast, began offering portrait sessions and selling prints of his landscape photos. His work was featured in local galleries and online, providing him with a rewarding income stream.

b. Leveraging Technology

Technology can amplify your efforts to turn hobbies into profitable ventures. From online marketplaces to digital marketing tools, technology provides the resources needed to reach a broader audience and streamline your business operations.

Tech Tools for Hobby Entrepreneurs:

- **E-Commerce Platforms:** Websites like Etsy, Shopify, and Amazon Handmade make it easy to sell products online.
- **Social Media Marketing:** Platforms like Instagram, Facebook, and Pinterest are powerful tools for showcasing your work and connecting with potential customers.
- **Digital Payment Solutions:** Services like PayPal, Square, and Stripe facilitate secure and convenient transactions.
- **Online Learning:** Utilize online courses and tutorials to enhance your skills and learn new business strategies.

Example:
Linda, who loves baking, started a home-based bakery selling cookies and cakes through a Shopify store. By using Instagram to showcase her creations and accepting orders online, Linda expanded her customer base beyond her local community, significantly increasing her sales.

3. Balancing Work with Leisure in the Golden Years

a. Prioritizing Work-Life Balance

Maintaining a healthy balance between work and leisure is essential for enjoying your retirement. While earning additional income is beneficial, it's equally important to allocate time for relaxation, hobbies, and spending time with loved ones.

Strategies for Balancing Work and Leisure:

- **Set Clear Boundaries:** Define specific work hours and stick to them to ensure that work does not encroach on your personal time.
- **Schedule Leisure Activities:** Prioritize activities that bring you joy and relaxation, such as traveling, gardening, or spending time with family.

- **Practice Self-Care:** Take care of your physical and mental well-being through regular exercise, healthy eating, and mindfulness practices.
- **Delegate When Necessary:** If your business grows, consider delegating tasks to employees or outsourcing certain aspects to maintain a manageable workload.

b. Integrating Work with Personal Interests

One of the joys of retirement is the ability to integrate work seamlessly with personal interests. This integration can lead to greater satisfaction and a sense of purpose.

Examples:

- **Teaching and Mentoring:** If you have expertise in a particular field, consider teaching classes or mentoring younger professionals, combining your passion for education with the joy of sharing knowledge.
- **Travel-Based Ventures:** For those who love to travel, starting a travel blog or offering travel planning services can merge work with the pleasure of exploring new places.
- **Fitness and Wellness:** If you're passionate about fitness, consider becoming a personal trainer or leading yoga classes, promoting both your well-being and that of others.

c. Embracing Flexibility

Flexibility is key to enjoying a balanced and fulfilling retirement. Being able to adjust your work commitments based on your energy levels and personal interests ensures that work remains a source of joy rather than stress.

Tips for Embracing Flexibility:

- **Flexible Scheduling:** Choose work opportunities that allow you to set your own hours and adjust them as needed.
- **Variety in Activities:** Engage in different types of work to keep things interesting and prevent burnout.
- **Listen to Your Body:** Pay attention to your physical and mental health, and adjust your workload accordingly to maintain overall well-being.

Example:
Emma, a retired teacher, started offering evening tutoring sessions while dedicating her mornings to painting and gardening. This flexible schedule allowed her to earn extra income without sacrificing her personal interests, creating a harmonious balance between work and leisure.

4. Success Stories: Real-Life Examples

a. Grace's Handmade Jewelry Business

Grace, a 70-year-old retired librarian, turned her love for jewelry-making into a thriving business. She began by crafting unique pieces in her home and selling them at local craft fairs. Encouraged by the positive feedback, Grace launched an online store on Etsy. By utilizing social media to showcase her creations and engaging with customers, Grace expanded her reach nationally. Today, her handmade jewelry business not only provides a steady income but also connects her with a community of fellow artisans and enthusiasts.

b. Robert's Consulting Firm

Robert, a 68-year-old retired civil engineer, founded a consulting firm specializing in sustainable building practices. Drawing on his decades of experience, Robert offers expert advice to new construction projects focused on environmental sustainability. His firm quickly gained a reputation for excellence, allowing him to work on meaningful projects that align with his values. Robert's consulting business provides him with substantial income while allowing him to contribute to a cause he is passionate about.

5. Tips for Success in New Ventures

a. Start Small and Scale Gradually

Beginning with a manageable workload allows you to test the waters and make adjustments without feeling overwhelmed. As you gain confidence and experience, you can gradually expand your efforts.

b. Network and Connect

Building a network of contacts can provide support, advice, and opportunities for collaboration. Attend local business events, join online communities, and connect with others who share your interests.

c. Stay Organized and Manage Time Effectively

Effective time management ensures that you can balance work and leisure without feeling stressed. Use tools like planners, calendars, and task management apps to stay organized and prioritize your activities.

d. Seek Continuous Learning

Embrace lifelong learning by taking courses, attending workshops, and staying informed about trends in your field.

Continuous learning enhances your skills and keeps your ventures innovative and competitive.

Crafting a Fulfilling Retirement

Embarking on new ventures in retirement opens the door to financial growth, personal fulfillment, and a sense of purpose. Whether through part-time work, entrepreneurship, or monetizing hobbies, there are countless ways to earn income on your terms. By prioritizing balance, embracing flexibility, and leveraging your passions, you can create a retirement that is both financially secure and deeply rewarding.

Key Takeaways:

- **Explore Flexible Work Options:** Part-time jobs and entrepreneurial ventures offer flexible ways to earn income while maintaining a balanced lifestyle.
- **Monetize Your Passions:** Turning hobbies into profitable endeavors can provide both financial benefits and personal satisfaction.
- **Maintain Work-Life Balance:** Prioritize leisure and self-care to ensure a fulfilling and stress-free retirement.
- **Leverage Technology and Networks:** Utilize online tools and build supportive networks to enhance your business efforts.
- **Start Small and Grow Gradually:** Begin with manageable projects and scale your efforts as you gain confidence and experience.

Action Steps:

1. **Identify Your Interests:** Reflect on your passions and skills to determine potential income-generating opportunities.

2. **Research Opportunities:** Explore part-time work options, entrepreneurial ventures, and ways to monetize your hobbies.
3. **Create a Plan:** Develop a clear plan outlining your goals, steps to achieve them, and how to balance work with leisure.
4. **Take the First Step:** Begin small by testing your ideas and gradually expanding as you gain confidence and experience.
5. **Stay Flexible and Adaptable:** Be open to adjusting your plans based on your experiences and changing circumstances.

Chapter 7: Living Well for Less

Achieving Financial Freedom Without Compromising Quality of Life

Retirement is a time to enjoy the fruits of your labor, but it often comes with the challenge of making your savings stretch further. Living well for less doesn't mean sacrificing the things you love; it's about adopting smart strategies to manage expenses while maintaining a fulfilling and joyful lifestyle. This chapter explores effective ways to reduce costs without compromising quality, offering practical tips on downsizing, smart shopping, and embracing a more meaningful, less materialistic life.

1. Strategies for Reducing Expenses Without Sacrificing Quality of Life

a. Create a Realistic Budget

A well-structured budget is the foundation of financial management. It allows you to track your income and expenses, identify areas where you can cut costs, and ensure that your spending aligns with your priorities.

Steps to Create a Budget:

1. **List Your Income Sources:** Include Social Security, pensions, retirement accounts, part-time work, and any other sources of income.
2. **Track Your Expenses:** Categorize your spending into essentials (housing, utilities, groceries) and non-essentials (entertainment, dining out).

3. **Set Spending Limits:** Allocate specific amounts to each category based on your income and financial goals.
4. **Monitor and Adjust:** Regularly review your budget to ensure you're staying on track and make adjustments as needed.

b. Prioritize Needs Over Wants

Distinguishing between needs and wants helps you focus on essential expenses while minimizing discretionary spending. This doesn't mean eliminating enjoyment but rather making intentional choices about where to allocate your resources.

Tips to Prioritize Needs:

- **Essentials First:** Ensure that your basic needs—housing, utilities, healthcare, and food—are fully covered before allocating funds to non-essentials.
- **Evaluate Subscriptions:** Cancel subscriptions and memberships that you no longer use or find value in.
- **Mindful Spending:** Before making a purchase, ask yourself if it truly enhances your life or if it's an impulsive desire.

2. Tips on Downsizing, Smart Shopping, and Cost-Effective Living

a. Downsizing Your Living Space

Reducing the size of your home can significantly lower your expenses, from mortgage or rent payments to utility bills and maintenance costs. Downsizing also simplifies your life by reducing the amount of space you need to manage.

Steps to Downsize:

1. **Assess Your Needs:** Determine the minimum space you require based on your lifestyle and activities.
2. **Sell or Donate Unnecessary Items:** Clear out belongings that you no longer need or use. This not only reduces clutter but can also provide additional funds.
3. **Choose a Suitable Location:** Opt for a location that offers lower living costs while still meeting your needs for accessibility and amenities.
4. **Embrace Multi-Functional Spaces:** Select a home with flexible spaces that can serve multiple purposes, maximizing functionality without increasing size.

b. Smart Shopping Practices

Adopting smart shopping habits can lead to substantial savings over time. It's about being strategic and intentional with your purchases to get the best value for your money.

Smart Shopping Tips:

- **Plan Your Meals:** Creating a weekly meal plan helps avoid impulse buys and reduces food waste.
- **Use Coupons and Discounts:** Take advantage of coupons, discount codes, and sales to lower your grocery and household expenses.
- **Buy in Bulk:** Purchasing non-perishable items in bulk can reduce the cost per unit and save money in the long run.
- **Compare Prices:** Use price comparison tools and apps to find the best deals on the items you need.

c. Embracing Cost-Effective Living

Living cost-effectively involves making lifestyle choices that reduce expenses without diminishing your quality of life. It's about finding balance and making conscious decisions that align with your financial goals.

Cost-Effective Living Strategies:

- **Energy Efficiency:** Implement energy-saving measures such as using LED bulbs, installing programmable thermostats, and unplugging electronics when not in use to reduce utility bills.
- **Public Transportation:** Utilize public transportation, carpooling, or biking instead of owning and maintaining a vehicle to save on transportation costs.
- **DIY Projects:** Take on do-it-yourself projects for home maintenance, repairs, and improvements to save money on professional services.
- **Gardening:** Grow your own vegetables and herbs to save on grocery bills and enjoy fresh, homegrown produce.

3. Embracing a Lifestyle That Prioritizes Fulfillment Over Materialism

Shifting your focus from material possessions to experiences and personal fulfillment can lead to a more satisfying and less financially burdensome retirement.

a. Focus on Experiences

Investing in experiences rather than things can enhance your quality of life and create lasting memories without the ongoing costs associated with material possessions.

Ideas for Experience-Focused Living:

- **Travel:** Explore new places, whether locally or internationally, to broaden your horizons and enjoy new cultures.

- **Hobbies and Interests:** Dedicate time to hobbies that bring you joy and fulfillment, such as painting, hiking, or playing a musical instrument.
- **Social Activities:** Engage in social activities and community events to build connections and maintain a vibrant social life.

b. Cultivate Relationships

Strong relationships with family, friends, and community members contribute significantly to your emotional well-being and overall satisfaction in retirement.

Ways to Cultivate Relationships:

- **Stay Connected:** Regularly communicate with family and friends through phone calls, visits, or virtual meetings.
- **Join Clubs and Groups:** Participate in clubs, groups, or organizations that align with your interests to meet new people and build meaningful connections.
- **Volunteer:** Volunteering for causes you care about not only helps others but also provides a sense of purpose and community involvement.

c. Practice Minimalism

Adopting a minimalist approach means living with fewer possessions and focusing on what truly matters. This can lead to financial savings, reduced stress, and a more organized living space.

Minimalism Tips:

- **Declutter Regularly:** Periodically review and declutter your belongings to keep only what you need and value.

- **Quality Over Quantity:** Invest in high-quality items that last longer and provide greater satisfaction than numerous lower-quality alternatives.
- **Mindful Purchasing:** Before making a purchase, consider its necessity and how it aligns with your values and lifestyle goals.

4. Real-Life Examples: Living Well for Less

a. Betty's Smart Budgeting

Betty, a 70-year-old retired librarian, transformed her financial situation by implementing a strict budget. She tracked her expenses meticulously, identified areas where she could cut costs, and redirected those savings toward her retirement fund. By prioritizing needs over wants and avoiding unnecessary expenses, Betty was able to maintain her comfortable lifestyle while ensuring her savings lasted longer.

b. George's Downsizing Journey

George, a 68-year-old retired teacher, decided to downsize from his large family home to a smaller, more manageable condo. The move significantly reduced his housing costs, including mortgage payments, utilities, and maintenance expenses. Additionally, George sold his excess belongings, generating extra income that he invested to secure his financial future.

c. Linda's Minimalist Lifestyle

Linda, age 65, embraced minimalism by decluttering her home and focusing on experiences over material possessions. She sold unnecessary items, simplified her living space, and redirected her savings toward travel and hobbies. This shift not only reduced her expenses but also enhanced her overall happiness and fulfillment in retirement.

5. Tips for Sustaining Cost-Effective Living

a. Regular Financial Check-Ups

Periodically reviewing your financial situation ensures that your strategies remain effective and aligned with your goals. It allows you to make necessary adjustments based on changes in income, expenses, or personal circumstances.

How to Conduct Financial Check-Ups:

- **Review Your Budget:** Assess whether you're sticking to your budget and identify any areas needing adjustment.
- **Evaluate Savings and Investments:** Ensure your savings and investments are on track to meet your retirement goals.
- **Adjust Spending Habits:** Make changes to your spending habits as needed to maintain financial stability.

b. Stay Informed and Educated

Continuously educating yourself about personal finance and cost-effective living strategies can help you make informed decisions and adapt to changing circumstances.

Ways to Stay Informed:

- **Read Books and Articles:** Explore literature on personal finance, budgeting, and minimalist living.
- **Attend Workshops and Seminars:** Participate in educational events focused on financial management and cost-saving techniques.

- **Engage with Online Communities:** Join forums and social media groups where you can exchange tips and experiences with others.

c. Embrace Creativity and Innovation

Finding creative solutions to everyday challenges can lead to significant savings and enhance your quality of life.

Creative Cost-Saving Ideas:

- **Repurpose Items:** Find new uses for items you already own instead of purchasing new ones.
- **Home Gardening:** Grow your own vegetables and herbs to save on grocery bills and enjoy fresh produce.
- **DIY Repairs and Projects:** Learn basic repair skills to maintain your home and belongings without hiring professionals.

Living a Fulfilling and Cost-Effective Retirement

Living well for less is entirely achievable with the right strategies and mindset. By implementing effective budgeting, adopting smart shopping habits, and embracing a minimalist lifestyle, you can reduce expenses without sacrificing quality of life. Prioritizing fulfillment over materialism not only enhances your financial security but also enriches your retirement years with meaningful experiences and strong relationships.

Key Takeaways:

- **Create and Stick to a Budget:** Track your income and expenses to manage your finances effectively.
- **Downsize Wisely:** Reduce your living space and expenses without compromising on comfort.

- **Adopt Smart Shopping Practices:** Be intentional with your purchases to maximize value and minimize costs.
- **Embrace Minimalism:** Focus on what truly matters to enhance your quality of life.
- **Prioritize Fulfillment:** Invest in experiences and relationships over material possessions to achieve a more satisfying retirement.

**Action Steps

1. **Assess Your Current Expenses:** Identify areas where you can reduce costs without impacting your quality of life.
2. **Implement Downsizing Strategies:** Consider if downsizing your home or decluttering can help lower your expenses.
3. **Adopt Smart Shopping Habits:** Use coupons, buy in bulk, and prioritize needs over wants in your purchasing decisions.
4. **Focus on Experiences:** Allocate more of your budget towards activities and relationships that bring you joy and fulfillment.
5. **Monitor and Adjust:** Regularly review your financial plan to ensure it continues to meet your needs and goals.

By embracing these strategies, you can enjoy a financially secure and fulfilling retirement, living well for less while cherishing the moments that matter most.

Reflective Questions:

1. **What areas of my budget can be adjusted to reduce expenses without affecting my quality of life?**
2. **How can I incorporate more experiences and meaningful activities into my retirement?**

3. What steps can I take to downsize my living space effectively?
4. Which of my hobbies or passions could be turned into cost-effective or income-generating activities?
5. How can I maintain a balance between saving money and enjoying my retirement years?

Chapter 8: Your Support Network: Resources to Help You Thrive

Building a Strong Foundation for a Fulfilling Retirement

Retirement marks a significant transition in life, bringing both opportunities and challenges. While financial planning and smart investments are crucial, the importance of a robust support network cannot be overstated. A strong network provides not only financial assistance but also emotional support, companionship, and access to valuable resources that can enhance your quality of life. This chapter explores the various organizations and programs available to seniors, how to access community resources and support groups, and the critical role that a support network plays in ensuring a thriving retirement.

1. Organizations and Programs Offering Assistance to Seniors

Numerous organizations and programs are dedicated to supporting seniors in various aspects of their lives, from financial assistance and healthcare to social engagement and personal development. Understanding these resources can significantly enhance your retirement experience.

a. Government Programs

1. Social Security Administration (SSA)

- **Overview:** SSA administers Social Security benefits, which are a primary source of income for many retirees.
- **Services:** Provides retirement benefits, disability benefits, and survivors' benefits.
- **Access:** Apply online at the SSA website, visit a local SSA office, or call their helpline for assistance.

2. Medicare

- **Overview:** Medicare is a federal health insurance program for individuals aged 65 and older.
- **Parts:**
    - *Part A:* Hospital insurance.
    - *Part B:* Medical insurance.
    - *Part C:* Medicare Advantage plans.
    - *Part D:* Prescription drug coverage.
- **Access:** Enroll during the Initial Enrollment Period around your 65th birthday. Visit the Medicare website for more information.

3. Supplemental Security Income (SSI)

- **Overview:** SSI provides financial assistance to low-income seniors and individuals with disabilities.
- **Services:** Offers monthly payments to help meet basic needs for food, clothing, and shelter.
- **Access:** Apply through the SSA website, local SSA offices, or by phone.

b. Non-Profit Organizations

1. AARP (American Association of Retired Persons)

- **Overview:** AARP is a membership organization focused on empowering people aged 50 and older.
- **Services:** Offers advocacy, discounts on various products and services, educational resources, and social activities.
- **Access:** Join as a member on the AARP website to access benefits and resources.

2. Meals on Wheels

- **Overview:** Provides nutritious meals to seniors who are homebound or have limited access to food.
- **Services:** Delivers meals, offers companionship, and monitors the well-being of recipients.
- **Access:** Contact your local Meals on Wheels program through their website or local senior centers.

3. National Council on Aging (NCOA)

- **Overview:** NCOA works to improve the lives of millions of older adults through advocacy, programs, and services.
- **Services:** Offers resources on health, economic security, and independent living.
- **Access:** Visit the NCOA website to explore programs and find local affiliates.

c. Community-Based Organizations

1. Local Senior Centers

- **Overview:** Senior centers provide a variety of services, including recreational activities, educational programs, and social events.
- **Services:** Offer classes, exercise programs, meal services, and opportunities for socialization.
- **Access:** Locate your nearest senior center through local government websites or community directories.

2. Area Agencies on Aging (AAA)

- **Overview:** AAAs are local organizations that coordinate services for older adults within their communities.
- **Services:** Provide information on benefits, home care services, transportation, and support groups.
- **Access:** Find your local AAA through the Eldercare Locator website or by contacting your state's Department of Health and Human Services.

3. United Way

- **Overview:** United Way partners with local organizations to address community needs, including those of seniors.
- **Services:** Offers programs related to health, education, financial stability, and emergency assistance.
- **Access:** Visit the United Way website to find local chapters and available services.

d. Healthcare Organizations

1. Kaiser Permanente's Senior Programs

- **Overview:** Kaiser Permanente offers specialized programs to support the health and well-being of seniors.
- **Services:** Includes preventive care, chronic disease management, and wellness programs.
- **Access:** Enroll through Kaiser Permanente's website or contact a local office.

2. American Heart Association (AHA) Senior Programs

- **Overview:** AHA provides resources and programs focused on cardiovascular health for seniors.
- **Services:** Offers educational materials, support groups, and community events.
- **Access:** Explore senior-specific resources on the AHA website or participate in local AHA events.

2. Accessing Community Resources and Support Groups

Accessing the right resources and joining support groups can significantly enhance your retirement experience by providing assistance, fostering connections, and promoting personal growth.

a. How to Find and Access Resources

1. Online Directories and Databases

- **Eldercare Locator:** A public service of the U.S. Administration on Aging that connects older adults and their caregivers with local resources. Accessible through

the Eldercare Locator website or by calling 1-800-677-1116.
- **Benefits.gov:** Provides information on federal benefits and assistance programs for seniors. Visit the Benefits.gov website to explore eligibility and application processes.

2. Local Libraries and Community Centers

- **Services:** Libraries often host informational sessions, workshops, and have bulletin boards with listings of local resources.
- **Access:** Visit your local library or community center and inquire about available programs and resources for seniors.

3. Healthcare Providers

- **Role:** Doctors, nurses, and other healthcare professionals can refer you to relevant programs and support services.
- **Access:** Speak with your primary care physician or healthcare provider about available resources tailored to your needs.

b. Joining Support Groups

1. Emotional Support Groups

- **Purpose:** Provide a safe space to share experiences, challenges, and triumphs with peers who understand your situation.
- **Benefits:** Offer emotional relief, reduce feelings of isolation, and foster a sense of community.
- **Access:** Find local support groups through AAAs, senior centers, or organizations like the National Alliance on Mental Illness (NAMI).

2. Financial Support Groups

- **Purpose:** Focus on financial planning, budgeting, and sharing strategies to manage finances effectively.
- **Benefits:** Gain insights from others, receive practical advice, and stay motivated to achieve financial goals.
- **Access:** Look for financial workshops and support groups at local community centers, libraries, or through organizations like the NCOA.

3. Health and Wellness Groups

- **Purpose:** Promote physical and mental health through group activities, exercise classes, and wellness workshops.
- **Benefits:** Improve overall health, build social connections, and stay active.
- **Access:** Join fitness classes, yoga groups, or wellness workshops offered by senior centers, gyms, or healthcare organizations.

c. Leveraging Technology for Connection

1. Virtual Support Groups

- **Overview:** Online platforms allow you to join support groups and participate in discussions from the comfort of your home.
- **Benefits:** Access to a broader network, flexibility in scheduling, and convenience.
- **Access:** Platforms like Zoom, Facebook Groups, and specialized websites offer virtual support group options.

2. Social Media and Online Communities

- **Overview:** Social media platforms and online forums provide opportunities to connect with other seniors, share experiences, and access resources.
- **Benefits:** Stay connected with friends and family, meet new people with similar interests, and stay informed about relevant topics.
- **Access:** Join groups on Facebook, participate in Reddit communities, or engage in online forums dedicated to senior interests.

3. The Importance of Building a Network for Financial and Emotional Support

A strong support network is invaluable in retirement, offering both tangible assistance and emotional companionship. Building and maintaining such a network can lead to a more secure and fulfilling retirement.

a. Financial Support

1. Sharing Resources and Information

- **Benefit:** Exchange information about financial opportunities, such as grants, loans, and investment strategies.
- **Example:** Joining a financial support group where members share tips on budgeting, saving, and investing can enhance your financial literacy and help you make informed decisions.

2. Collaborative Opportunities

- **Benefit:** Partner with others for joint ventures, such as starting a small business or investing in real estate.

- **Example:** Networking with fellow retirees interested in entrepreneurship can lead to collaborative projects that pool resources and expertise, increasing the likelihood of success.

3. Access to Professional Advice

- **Benefit:** Connect with financial advisors, legal experts, and other professionals who can provide personalized guidance.
- **Example:** Attending workshops or seminars hosted by financial experts allows you to ask questions and receive tailored advice on managing your finances effectively.

b. Emotional Support

1. Reducing Isolation and Loneliness

- **Benefit:** Building connections with peers helps combat feelings of isolation, which are common in retirement.
- **Example:** Participating in social clubs, hobby groups, or volunteer organizations fosters meaningful relationships and a sense of belonging.

2. Enhancing Mental Health

- **Benefit:** Emotional support from a strong network contributes to better mental health and overall well-being.
- **Example:** Engaging in regular social activities and maintaining close relationships can reduce stress, anxiety, and the risk of depression.

3. Providing Encouragement and Motivation

- **Benefit:** A supportive network can motivate you to pursue new goals, stay active, and maintain a positive outlook.
- **Example:** Friends and peers can encourage you to try new activities

4. Practical Tips for Building and Maintaining Your Support Network

a. Get Involved in Community Activities

1. Attend Local Events

- **Benefit:** Participating in community events helps you meet new people and stay engaged.
- **Example:** Attend local fairs, farmers markets, or cultural festivals to connect with others and build relationships.

2. Volunteer Your Time

- **Benefit:** Volunteering provides a sense of purpose and an opportunity to give back while meeting like-minded individuals.
- **Example:** Join a local charity organization, community center, or hospital volunteer program to contribute your time and skills.

b. Pursue Lifelong Learning

1. Enroll in Classes and Workshops

- **Benefit:** Learning new skills or pursuing interests can expand your network and keep your mind active.
- **Example:** Take a class at a community college, senior center, or online platform to meet others with similar interests.

2. Join Book Clubs or Discussion Groups

- **Benefit:** Engaging in intellectual discussions fosters connections and stimulates cognitive function.
- **Example:** Participate in a local book club or online discussion group to share ideas and enjoy meaningful conversations.

c. Stay Connected with Family and Friends

1. Regular Communication

- **Benefit:** Maintaining strong relationships with family and friends provides a stable support system.
- **Example:** Schedule regular phone calls, video chats, or visits to stay connected and support each other.

2. Plan Social Gatherings

- **Benefit:** Organizing gatherings fosters a sense of community and strengthens bonds.
- **Example:** Host monthly potlucks, game nights, or outing trips with friends and family to create lasting memories.

d. Utilize Technology to Enhance Connections

1. Leverage Social Media Platforms

- **Benefit:** Social media allows you to stay in touch with a broader network and discover new connections.
- **Example:** Use Facebook, Instagram, or LinkedIn to connect with old friends, join interest-based groups, and participate in online communities.

2. Participate in Online Forums and Groups

- **Benefit:** Online forums provide a space to discuss common interests, share experiences, and seek advice.
- **Example:** Join forums on platforms like Reddit, Quora, or specialized websites focused on senior interests and issues.

e. Seek Professional Networking Opportunities

1. Attend Industry Conferences and Seminars

- **Benefit:** Professional events offer opportunities to network with experts and peers in your field.
- **Example:** Attend seminars on retirement planning, healthcare, or entrepreneurship to meet professionals and gain valuable insights.

2. Join Professional Associations

- **Benefit:** Professional associations provide resources, networking opportunities, and support tailored to your expertise.
- **Example:** If you have a background in education, join an association for retired educators to connect with former colleagues and access specialized resources.

5. Leveraging Available Resources to Enhance Your Network

a. Financial Assistance Programs

1. Low-Income Home Energy Assistance Program (LIHEAP)

- **Overview:** LIHEAP helps eligible low-income households with their heating and cooling energy costs.
- **Benefit:** Reduces monthly utility expenses, freeing up funds for other necessities.

- **Access:** Apply through your local LIHEAP office or community agency.

2. Supplemental Nutrition Assistance Program (SNAP)

- **Overview:** SNAP provides financial assistance for purchasing food.
- **Benefit:** Ensures access to nutritious meals without straining your budget.
- **Access:** Apply online through your state's SNAP website or visit a local SNAP office.

b. Health and Wellness Programs

1. SilverSneakers

- **Overview:** A fitness program specifically designed for older adults.
- **Benefit:** Provides access to gym memberships, fitness classes, and wellness programs at no additional cost or at a reduced rate.
- **Access:** Check if your Medicare Advantage plan includes SilverSneakers or enroll directly through their website.

2. Chronic Disease Self-Management Program (CDSMP)

- **Overview:** A program that helps individuals manage chronic health conditions.
- **Benefit:** Provides tools and strategies to improve health outcomes and reduce healthcare costs.
- **Access:** Participate in classes offered by local community centers, hospitals, or through the NCOA.

c. Educational and Skill Development Resources

1. SeniorNet

- **Overview:** A non-profit organization dedicated to providing older adults with computer and internet education.
- **Benefit:** Enhances digital literacy, enabling you to access online resources, connect with others, and manage your finances.
- **Access:** Join local SeniorNet groups or participate in online classes offered through their website.

2. Coursera and edX

- **Overview:** Online learning platforms offering courses from top universities and institutions.
- **Benefit:** Provides opportunities to learn new skills, pursue interests, and engage in lifelong learning.
- **Access:** Enroll in courses through the Coursera or edX websites, many of which are free or available at a low cost.

6. The Role of Emotional Support in Financial Well-Being

Emotional support is intertwined with financial well-being. Stress and anxiety related to financial concerns can negatively impact your mental health, while a strong support network can provide reassurance and practical assistance.

a. Reducing Financial Stress

1. Open Communication

- **Benefit:** Discussing financial concerns with trusted individuals can alleviate stress and provide new perspectives.
- **Example:** Share your financial goals and challenges with a spouse, family member, or close friend to receive support and advice.

2. Mindfulness and Stress-Reduction Techniques

- **Benefit:** Practices like meditation, yoga, and deep breathing can help manage stress related to financial worries.
- **Example:** Incorporate daily meditation or join a yoga class to maintain mental and emotional balance.

b. Enhancing Overall Well-Being

1. Social Engagement

- **Benefit:** Regular social interactions contribute to a sense of purpose and belonging, enhancing overall well-being.
- **Example:** Join clubs, attend community events, or participate in volunteer activities to stay socially active.

2. Pursuing Meaningful Activities

- **Benefit:** Engaging in activities that you find meaningful and fulfilling can improve your mental health and happiness.
- **Example:** Dedicate time to hobbies, volunteer work, or projects that align with your values and interests.

c. Building Resilience Through Support

1. Learning from Others

- **Benefit:** Hearing stories and experiences from peers can provide valuable insights and inspire resilience.
- **Example:** Participate in support groups where members share their financial journeys and coping strategies.

2. Seeking Professional Help When Needed

- **Benefit:** Professional counselors and therapists can offer strategies to manage emotional challenges related to retirement and finances.
- **Example:** Schedule regular sessions with a therapist to address any lingering anxieties or emotional concerns.

7. Maintaining and Strengthening Your Support Network

Building a support network is an ongoing process that requires effort and intentionality. Here are strategies to ensure your network remains strong and supportive.

a. Regular Communication

1. Stay in Touch

- **Benefit:** Consistent communication helps maintain and strengthen relationships.
- **Example:** Schedule regular phone calls, video chats, or meet-ups with friends and family to stay connected.

2. Share Your Experiences

- **Benefit:** Sharing your experiences fosters mutual understanding and support.
- **Example:** Join a storytelling group or a blog where you can share your retirement journey and learn from others.

b. Expanding Your Network

1. Attend New Activities

- **Benefit:** Trying new activities can introduce you to different people and expand your social circle.
- **Example:** Take up a new hobby, join a dance class, or participate in a local sports league to meet new individuals.

2. Volunteer in Diverse Roles

- **Benefit:** Volunteering in various capacities exposes you to different communities and broadens your network.
- **Example:** Volunteer at a local hospital, animal shelter, or community garden to connect with diverse groups of people.

c. Leveraging Technology

1. Utilize Social Media

- **Benefit:** Social media platforms facilitate easy and ongoing communication with a broad network.
- **Example:** Use Facebook to join groups related to your interests, participate in discussions, and stay updated on community events.

2. Participate in Virtual Events

- **Benefit:** Virtual events provide opportunities to connect with others without geographical limitations.
- **Example:** Attend online webinars, virtual meet-ups, or live-streamed classes to engage with a wider audience.

d. Investing Time and Effort

1. Be Proactive

- **Benefit:** Actively seeking out connections ensures your network remains dynamic and supportive.
- **Example:** Reach out to old friends, join new groups, and attend community events regularly.

2. Offer Support to Others

- **Benefit:** Providing support to others strengthens reciprocal relationships and builds trust.
- **Example:** Offer to help a neighbor with errands, mentor a younger individual, or participate in community initiatives.

8. Real-Life Examples: Thriving with a Support Network

a. Susan's Engagement with Local Organizations

Susan, a 67-year-old retired teacher, leveraged her involvement in local organizations to build a robust support network. By joining the local chapter of AARP and participating in community center activities, Susan connected with peers who shared her interests in gardening and education. These connections provided her with emotional support, friendship, and access to valuable resources, enhancing her overall quality of life.

b. David's Use of Online Communities

David, age 70, found solace and support through online communities after his spouse passed away. By joining forums and participating in virtual support groups, David met individuals who understood his grief and offered practical advice on financial management and emotional healing. This online network became a cornerstone of his support system, helping him navigate his new life with confidence and companionship.

c. Linda's Volunteer Work

Linda, a 65-year-old retired nurse, built her support network through volunteer work at a local hospital and community health clinics. Her volunteering not only provided her with a sense of purpose but also connected her with healthcare professionals and fellow volunteers who became close friends. These relationships offered both financial advice and emotional support, contributing to Linda's thriving retirement.

9. Final Thoughts: Empowering Yourself Through a Strong Support Network

Building and maintaining a strong support network is a vital component of a thriving retirement. Organizations and programs dedicated to seniors offer a wealth of resources and assistance, while community resources and support groups provide the emotional and practical support needed to navigate the challenges of retirement. By actively engaging with these resources and fostering meaningful relationships, you can enhance your financial security, improve your mental and emotional well-being, and enjoy a fulfilling and vibrant retirement.

Key Takeaways:

- **Utilize Available Resources:** Take advantage of government programs, non-profit organizations, and community-based services tailored to senior needs.
- **Join Support Groups:** Engage in emotional, financial, and health-focused support groups to build connections and gain valuable insights.
- **Leverage Technology:** Use online platforms to expand your network, stay connected, and access virtual resources.
- **Prioritize Relationships:** Focus on building and maintaining strong relationships with family, friends, and peers to provide both financial and emotional support.
- **Stay Proactive:** Continuously seek out new opportunities to engage, learn, and connect to ensure your support network remains dynamic and supportive.

Action Steps:

1. **Identify Key Resources:** Research and list organizations and programs that offer assistance to seniors in your area and online.
2. **Join Local and Online Groups:** Enroll in community centers, senior groups, and online forums to start building your support network.
3. **Engage Regularly:** Participate in events, volunteer activities, and support group meetings to maintain and strengthen your connections.
4. **Seek Professional Help:** Consult with financial advisors, counselors, and other professionals to enhance your financial and emotional well-being.
5. **Foster Meaningful Relationships:** Invest time and effort in building strong, supportive relationships that contribute to your overall happiness and security.

By embracing these strategies and leveraging the resources available, you can create a robust support network that empowers you to thrive in your retirement years. Remember, the journey to a fulfilling retirement is not one you need to navigate alone—your support network is there to help you every step of the way.

Reflective Questions:

1. Which organizations and programs resonate most with your current needs, and how can you engage with them?
2. What steps can you take to connect with local community resources and support groups?
3. How can you leverage technology to expand and strengthen your support network?
4. What relationships in your life can you nurture to provide financial and emotional support?
5. How can you contribute to your support network to ensure it remains strong and mutually beneficial?

Conclusion: Stepping Confidently into the Future

Embracing a New Chapter with Confidence and Purpose

As you turn the final pages of this book, it's essential to reflect on the journey we've embarked upon together. *Retirement Reimagined: Empowering Strategies for Financial Freedom After 60* has been crafted to guide you through the evolving landscape of retirement, equipping you with the knowledge and tools necessary to thrive in your golden years. Let's revisit the key takeaways and look forward to the opportunities that await you.

Key Takeaways

1. Understanding the New Reality of Retirement

Retirement today is more dynamic and diverse than ever before. With longer life expectancies and shifting economic landscapes, it's crucial to approach this phase with flexibility and proactive planning. Embracing the realities of extended work life and the need for sustained financial health sets the foundation for a secure future.

2. Facing Financial Facts Without Fear

Honest assessment of your financial situation is the first step toward financial empowerment. By understanding your savings, managing expenses, and eliminating debt, you can build a robust financial base that supports your retirement dreams. Proactive financial planning transforms uncertainty into confidence.

3. Triumphs After 60: Stories of Success

Real-life stories of individuals who have successfully navigated their financial challenges serve as powerful reminders that it's never too late to make positive changes. These narratives inspire resilience, creativity, and the pursuit of new opportunities, demonstrating that financial security and personal fulfillment are attainable at any age.

4. Supercharging Your Savings: Proven Techniques

Smart investing, effective budgeting, and diligent debt management are essential strategies for maximizing your retirement funds. By diversifying investments, creating realistic budgets, and prioritizing debt elimination, you can enhance your financial stability and enjoy a more comfortable retirement.

5. Unlocking the Full Potential of Social Security and Medicare

Maximizing Social Security benefits and navigating Medicare complexities are critical for securing your financial and health needs. Strategic timing and coordination of these programs can significantly boost your income and ensure comprehensive healthcare coverage, providing peace of mind throughout your retirement.

6. New Ventures: Earning Income on Your Terms

Retirement offers the perfect opportunity to explore part-time work, entrepreneurial ventures, and turning hobbies into profitable endeavors. Balancing work with leisure allows you to stay active, engaged, and financially independent, enriching your retirement experience with purpose and passion.

7. Living Well for Less

Adopting cost-effective living strategies—such as downsizing, smart shopping, and embracing minimalism—enables you to reduce expenses without sacrificing quality of life. Prioritizing fulfillment over materialism leads to a more meaningful and financially sustainable retirement.

8. Your Support Network: Resources to Help You Thrive

Building a strong support network is vital for both financial and emotional well-being. Leveraging community resources, joining support groups, and maintaining meaningful relationships provide essential assistance and companionship, enhancing your overall retirement experience.

Encouraging Ongoing Action

The journey to a fulfilling retirement is ongoing, requiring continuous effort and adaptability. Here's how you can keep moving forward with confidence:

- **Stay Informed:** Keep up with financial news, retirement trends, and changes in social programs to make informed decisions.
- **Set and Review Goals:** Regularly revisit your financial and personal goals to ensure they align with your evolving needs and aspirations.
- **Seek Professional Advice:** Don't hesitate to consult financial advisors, tax professionals, and healthcare experts to refine your strategies and optimize your plans.
- **Engage in Lifelong Learning:** Continue to educate yourself through books, courses, and workshops to enhance your skills and knowledge.

- **Adapt and Innovate:** Be open to adjusting your plans as circumstances change, embracing new opportunities and overcoming challenges with resilience.

Reinforcing Empowerment and Self-Sufficiency

Empowerment comes from taking control of your financial and personal life. By applying the strategies and insights shared in this book, you can achieve self-sufficiency and independence, ensuring that you are well-prepared to handle whatever the future holds. Remember, your financial health is a reflection of your proactive choices and your commitment to securing a stable and enjoyable retirement.

Embracing Future Opportunities

Retirement is a time ripe with possibilities. Whether it's pursuing new hobbies, starting a business, traveling, or deepening relationships, the opportunities to enrich your life are endless. Embrace these opportunities with enthusiasm and an open mind, knowing that you have the tools and support to make the most of your retirement years.

Take the Leap

- **Pursue Your Passions:** Don't let age limit your dreams. Whether it's writing, painting, gardening, or any other passion, pursue it with vigor and dedication.
- **Stay Active and Engaged:** Physical activity and mental stimulation are crucial for maintaining health and happiness. Engage in regular exercise, participate in community activities, and keep your mind sharp through continuous learning.
- **Foster Relationships:** Invest in your relationships with family, friends, and community members. These

connections provide emotional support, joy, and a sense of belonging.
- **Give Back:** Volunteering and mentoring can provide a profound sense of purpose and fulfillment, allowing you to contribute to society and help others.

Final Inspiration

Your retirement is a new chapter, a time to redefine what it means to live well and achieve financial freedom. With the right mindset, strategies, and support, you can step confidently into the future, embracing every opportunity to create a life that is not only financially secure but also rich in experiences and personal satisfaction.

Remember: Empowerment and self-sufficiency are within your reach. By taking proactive steps today, you can build a retirement that reflects your values, fulfills your dreams, and ensures a prosperous and joyful future.

A Call to Action

As you close this book, let it be the beginning of your proactive journey toward a secure and fulfilling retirement. Take the insights and strategies you've gained, apply them to your unique situation, and continue seeking out new opportunities for growth and enrichment. Your future is bright, and with determination and the right support, you can achieve the financial freedom and personal fulfillment you deserve.

Stay Empowered. Stay Independent. Embrace the Future with Confidence.

www.ingramcontent.com/pod-product-compliance
Lightning Source LLC
Chambersburg PA
CBHW052055070526
44584CB00017B/2195